Dedicati

To my dearest, beloved spiritual grandfather Thay (Thich Nhat Hanh).

I am grateful for your true presence and feel deeply blessed to be guided by your beautiful wisdom and teachings of peace, love, and understanding.

You inspire millions of people throughout the world with your deep respect and love for life. We are all eternally grateful to you.

This book is a continuation of your loving, grateful heart.

With my deepest respect, love, and gratitude

Falguni

Contents

How to use this book   6

Introduction   7

The Natural World

    Generous Mother Earth   8

    The Miracle of Water   10

    All Creatures Great and Small   12

    The Sacred Tree   14

    The Love of Flowers   16

Celestial Wonders

    Sundance   18

    Moonshine   20

    Journey Creation of the Stars   22

Health & Wellness

    Breathe My Dear   24

    Nutritional Blessings   26

    Our Immune System Friends   28

    The Wellness of Illness   30

    A Good Night's Sleep   32

Joy of Life

    The Beauty of a Smile   34

    Laughter is the Best Medicine   36

    Life's Simple Pleasures   38

Weather

    Language of the Skies   40

    Raindance   42

New Beginnings

    A Voyage of Discovery   43

    Anything is Possible   44

    A Brand New Day   46

Family & Friends
  Continuation of our Ancestors 48
  Dear Friends 50

Inner Qualities
  My Spirit Within 52
  Seeds of Gratitude 54
  Doing My Bit 56

The Six Senses
  The Fragrance of Gratitude 57
  Music, the Voice of the Soul 58
  The Colours of the Sun 60
  The Sound of Silence 62
  A Sense of the World 64

Creative
  Stick-it Happy 66
  Scraps of Gratitude 67
  And the Award Goes To 68
  The Gratitude Jar 70
  The Alphabet Game 71
  A Picture Paints a Thousand Words 72
  Motion Pictures 74
  Wise Words 75
  Tree of Gratitude 76
  Pebble in My Hand 78
  Just a Little Note to Say ... 79

Environment
  Swept Away 79
  Reduce, Reuse & Recycle 80

Heart to Heart
  A Prayer of Thanks 82
  Gratitude Sharing 84
  I Wish You Well 86
  Heartfulness 88
  Speak from Your Heart 90
  Meaningful Conversations 92

Techie Tools

 Gadgets, Gizmos, and Tools 93
 Have you tried turning it off and on again? 94

Beliefs, Perceptions and Attitude

 Replacing an Ungrateful Thought 96
 A Room with a View 98
 An Attitude of Gratitude 100
 Believe or Not to Believe 102

Grateful Living

 A Warm Thanks 104
 Electric Dreams 105
 Home Sweet Home 106
 Love of Land and Country 107
 The Value of Money 108
 Freedom 110

The Human Body

 The Wonder of the Body 112
 The Amazing Duo 114
 A Journey of a Thousand Mile 115
 A Walk of Gratitude 116

Past, Present & Future

 One Hundred Gifts 118
 Timelessness of Gratitude 119
 Missing You 120
 My Aspirations for Gratitude 122
 Calendar Moments 123
 Step Back in Time 124
 No Mud, No Lotus 126
 The Memory of Written Words 128
 Time Traveller 130
 Ageless Spirit 132
 Visiting Your Past Self 134
 The Passage of Time 136
 Just Being 137
 The Beauty of Imperfection 138

Kindness

    Hands that Feed   139

    An Act of Kindness   140

    Speaking Kindly of Others   142

    Are you being Served?   144

    Watering the Flowers   146

    Remember the Good   148

    The Wisdom of Our Teachers   150

The Science of Gratitude

    Stress or Heal   152

    The Chemistry of Wellbeing   154

    The Two Minds   156

    Neurons that Fire together Wire together   158

    Placebo & Nocebo Effect   160

    The Grateful Gene   162

    The Mirror Effect   164

    Fountain of Youth   166

    Postcards from the Subconscious   168

    Focus & Attract   169

    Higher Vibrations   170

    Rewrite your History   172

    Serendipity & Synchronicity   174

Reflections

    Reflections of Gratitude   176

    The Miracle of Life   178

    I am grateful   179

Acknowledgments   180

About the Author   181

Bibliography & Further Reading   182

Recommended Websites   182

How to use this book

This book is useful for anyone who is looking for a positive path in their life; anyone who wishes to cultivate a deeper appreciation of life and live more fully in the present moment.

Each chapter of the book focuses on a particular area of gratitude and mindfulness practice. Within each chapter, there are many insights and creative practices that will hopefully inspire you to cultivate a grateful heart. The chapters are arranged in themed sections so that you can dip into them in any order depending on what kind of practice area you would like to focus on. The purpose of the book is to help you practice gratitude in a variety of creative ways, there is something for everyone. Explanations are repeated in a variety of different ways to help reinforce the teaching and practices. The key to symbols is a guide for you to dip into the book and choose a particular kind of practice you would like to try. Enjoy!

Key to Symbols

☺	Health & Wellness	🔥	Ritual / Ceremony
✏	Writing	🌍	Environment
🦋	Creative	❋	Nature
🧘	Meditation / Contemplation	♡	Relationships / Sharing
♫	Musical	🍎	Food
💧	Water	🐾	Wildlife
✡	Celestial	👁	Visualisation

Introduction

Gratitude means thankfulness, counting your blessings, noticing simple pleasures, and acknowledging everything that you receive. It means learning to live your life as if everything were a miracle, and being aware on a continuous basis of how much you've been given. Gratitude shifts your focus from what your life lacks to the abundance that is already present.

For many years I have practiced a variety of different holistic therapies from a diverse mix of traditions and cultures. I wanted something that would create a deep shift in my consciousness. My heart told me along the path that gratitude was the way. Gratitude merged everything I had learned into one whole practice. It is the thread that weaves itself through every spiritual practice.

This book was born out of a need to celebrate life within all its diversity of experiences, a desire to cultivate gratitude, thankfulness, and appreciation in creative ways so that we can develop an attitude that allows us to live in a state of grace. Every moment is filled with opportunities to fill our consciousness with feelings of gratitude. Every event in life becomes an opportunity to learn, to grow, and to expand our capacity to love.

Notice the magic that happens when you shift your awareness from the things you don't have to the things you do have. Happiness is a choice. Generating gratitude is a way of opening our eyes to the abundance that has always been there.

This book is my grateful love letter to life. Enjoy your wonderful journey of thankfulness. Become curious, be amazed, be inspired and inspire others, open your heart, be creative, be kind, create your own unique wonderful grateful journey, celebrate and feel blessed for this incredible gift of life.

Falguni Patel

Generous Mother Earth

"The Earth is our mother. Whatever befalls the Earth befalls the sons and daughters of the Earth. This we know. All things are connected. Humankind has not woven the web of life. We are but one thread within it. Whatever we do to the web we do to ourselves." Chief Seattle

The Planet Earth is our immensely beautiful home. Its nature is life-giving and very generous. We breathe in its clean fresh air, we drink from its fresh waters, we eat its bountiful food, we cultivate its land and we build homes from its land materials. The Earth provides us with the fuel to run the many types of machinery we use, to fuel our transport and to keep our homes warm. It provides the materials which make our clothing and it supplies the billions of gallons of water that are needed to process the billions of materials that we use in our lives. Most of what we use and consume on a daily basis remains the product of multitudes of interactions within nature. If we look deeply, every single thing that we use in our lives is provided in some way by the Earth. Earth's wondrous ecosystem and weather systems work beautifully to provide the right conditions for life to exist.

Beyond the physical tangible gifts that the natural world provides, we enjoy the benefits of its beauty and spirituality. Nature fills the human heart and spirit with love and wonder. When we are in nature we feel connected to it, we can feel its love and its beautiful healing energy. We need to be so grateful to the Planet Earth and what it gives us unconditionally, free-of-charge. It is important for us to understand our interconnectedness to everything around us. We exist only due to many conditions and gifts that the Earth provides. Many cultures have deep a respect for nature and the environment. Native Americans respected and considered their actions and how it would affect all of nature and life around them. Their communities would consider the effects as much as seven generations into the future. Many cultures perform sacred ceremonies and rituals to show their respect and gratitude to the Earth and all its elements. We can all learn to love, respect and be deeply grateful to our beautiful Mother Earth.

✳ Spend time in nature as often as you can. Get outside and enjoy beautiful Mother Earth. Observe and be present with Earth's many forms of life. Find ways to experience many different aspects and features of the natural wonders of Earth. Embrace being at one with nature.

✎ Write a love letter to the Earth. Tell Mother Earth what you love about her, how she helps you and how much you appreciate her gifts. You could choose something specific in nature that you are particularly grateful for. Write from your heart and send the Earth your love and appreciation. You can keep your love letter, read it out to someone or place it somewhere special in nature.

👁 Visualise yourself in a spacecraft in orbit around the Earth. Through a porthole you see the beautiful Planet Earth suspended in space. You see the vast oceans and huge expansive land. Visualise a bright ball of your grateful loving energy surrounding the Earth. You can also do this meditation while looking at an image of the Planet Earth. Feel in your heart how blessed you truly are to have such a generous and stunningly beautiful home.

✳ Lie face down on a patch of grass with your arms outstretched as though embracing the Earth. As you breathe in, absorb the beautiful vibrations of love from the Earth into your heart. As you breathe out, transmit your grateful loving energy from your heart deep into the Earth.

☸ Imagine yourself as a tree, flower, mountain, rock, waterfall, the sea, any life form in nature. Sense what it's like to be in its body, to live its life. What wisdom does it have for you?

◐ Invent your own sacred ceremony or ritual to show your gratitude and respect to the Earth. Be as creative as you like and get others involved. Concentrate on a particular aspect of nature or perform a ceremony or ritual that celebrates your gratitude to the whole of Mother Earth.

☸ Choose a natural feature or landscape to meditate on. Sit and be fully present with it. You can look up various pictures or videos or even choose a memory of a landscape. Spend time taking in its details. Become aware of how it makes you feel.

The Miracle of Water

"Nothing is softer or more flexible than water, yet nothing can resist it."
Lao Tsu

Fluid and transparent, soft and tough, clear and still, flexible and flowing; water is all around us in its different forms. About 70 percent of the Earth's surface is covered by water. It is found in the seas and oceans, in rivers and lakes, in icecaps and glaciers and deep within the ground. Water exists in the air as water vapour and within every cloud that hovers or passes over our Earth. It is a major part of our body, part of all our cells which make up all our tissues and organs. An average adult human body consists of approximately 70 percent water. Everything we eat contains water and we breathe in water from the air around us. It was water that allowed life to evolve on Earth; it is truly the most wondrous substance.

Water's lifecycle is never-ending. As the water falls from the clouds, the Earth gratefully uses up what it needs to survive and transports water back to the atmosphere to be recycled once again. When we drink water or eat foods that contain water, our body gratefully uses up just the right amount to nourish itself and eliminates the rest which then gets recycled. Water permeates everything it comes into contact with; passing, flowing, spreading or becoming part of whatever it touches. Over time water can mould and smooth rough rock surfaces and like air, it is soft and can travel and reach the hardest to reach or tiniest of places.

● Become mindful of all the places where water exists. Look carefully and you will find it everywhere. Some places are obvious, you can see it clearly, like streams, rivers, seas and oceans, the rain and the water that you use in your home. But some may be hidden, such as in food, in clouds, in people, in other animals, in yourself, in paper and in all the things that are made up of water or have used water to be made. Look around you now and see how many you can find. Stop and look more deeply at one of them; how has water contributed to its existence?

💧 Water is easily supplied through our taps straight into our home. We drink this water, we wash ourselves with it, we wash our dishes with it, we clean our house, we water our garden and much more. When you have a bath or shower, your whole body is covered with water. Feel how relaxing the water is on your skin, how it flows around your skin, its movement and refreshing nature. Listen to the splashing of the water around you, feel the joy that the water gives you and be grateful for it. Imagine yourself being blessed by the water while having a bath or shower. Do the same practice for when you are washing the dishes or cleaning your home with water; use your sense of sight, touch, and sound to immerse yourself into the whole renewing and refreshing experience.

💧 2.5 billion people, about a third of the world's population, do not have access to adequate sanitation. Feel grateful that water helps to flush away waste disposal every time you use and flush the toilet.

💧 Take a clear glass and fill it with water. Pick up the glass of water and really look at and be present with it. Bring your mind to settle on the water. What thoughts are arising in you? Mindfully take a sip; how does it feel in your mouth and on your tongue? How does the water feel as it flows down your throat and into your stomach? Feel how the water has become part of you. Close your eyes and focus on a particular part of your body. Visualise the tiny droplets of the water you are drinking passing into this body part and being absorbed by all its cells, nourishing and healing every part of it. 780 million people on our Planet do not have access to clean drinking water. Being aware of this fact, feel grateful for every drop of clean water that you are able to drink whenever you wish to or need to.

💧 Being around water in nature has wonderful therapeutic benefits. Meditate around water; rivers, lakes, streams, seas, oceans, waterfalls. You can also do this at home by watching, visualising or listening to recorded nature water sounds; it's very soothing when accompanied by soft music. Experience or visualise yourself floating on water, swimming in the sea, standing under a waterfall, placing your feet in a flowing stream, any experience you like involving water.

All Creatures Great and Small

"Our task must be to free ourselves by widening our circle of compassion to embrace all living creatures and the whole of nature and its beauty."
Albert Einstein

We share this Earth with so many different animals. Extraordinary creatures that live on the land, in the water, underground or fly in the air. The Earth provides a home, shelter, and food to every species on Earth. Wherever you live in the world, you will see some form of wildlife. Many creatures survive amongst the unpredictability that nature brings, in all weathers and conditions. Watching the way they live within nature is fascinating and opens our minds and hearts to understand how they survive. Many species have a symbiotic relationship with each other and with nature, where different species work together each benefiting from the relationship. The bees and flowers need each other to survive and reproduce. Dung Beatles use the faeces of other animals to lay their eggs in, feed on and make their home with. Many plant and tree species rely on creatures to reproduce, their seeds are eaten or are buried or transported to where they can spread and grow, and many animals rely on the plants and trees for food and shelter. Earthworms play an important role in breaking down and converting organic matter such as dead plant and animal material into a form that is usable for other organisms; their work is vital for the healthy functioning of the Earth's ecosystem.

🐾 Become mindful of the creatures around your environment. Choose one to observe on your own or with other people. It could be any wildlife in nature, your own pet or even someone else's pet. Just by noticing it and placing your awareness on it you acknowledge its existence. Cultivate your curiosity about the creature and generate gratefulness for sharing the environment together. Meditate on the role each living organism plays in sustaining the fabric of life within that area.

🐾 If you could be any creature on the Planet what type of creature would you be and why? What is your spirit animal?

❧ Observe the smaller creatures around you, such as insects, butterflies, worms or spiders, in nature or in your own home or garden. See how they have their own purpose in life, how they find their food, what they eat, how they work so well together, how they survive in their environment. Many people don't like spiders, but they are incredible creatures. Look at the delicate and intricate webs they spin. They have adapted to build webs and catch food under extraordinary circumstances. Their webs are built so strong that even heavy wind or rain can't break them. They work with great intelligence

❧ Do your bit to help animals. Get involved with animal charity organisations, volunteer; share your time and energy. Raise funds to help animal charities, spread the word to others on what help is needed, make a conscious choice to support the humane treatment of farm animals and eat humanely. Attract wildlife into your garden. Set up a bug hotel, put up bird feeders and a birdbath, plant flowers that will attract bees and butterflies, build a pond.

❧ Watching wildlife documentaries on television teaches us so much about other creatures. We are able to learn about their extraordinary lives, without leaving our home. Through the filmmaker's cameras, we see whole new worlds of the creatures we share the Planet with. Make an effort to sit down and watch a wildlife documentary and be grateful to be able to marvel and learn about different animals and their lives. Watch a documentary with someone else and talk about your favourite parts and what amazed you the most.

❧ Consider the special qualities that animals express; devotion, intelligence, cooperation, contentment, tireless joy, industrious self-reliance, determination, perseverance. Native people across many cultures believe that animals speak to us through their very natures. An encounter with an animal can point out qualities in us that we need to understand better. Choose a quality of a particular animal that you admire or respect and try and incorporate more of this quality into your own life and send them your gratitude for their teaching. We share this beautiful Planet with so many wonderful creatures; all wildlife has a story of life that we can learn from. Feel a renewed sense of respect for all living things.

The Sacred Tree

"Keep a green tree in your heart and perhaps the singing bird will come."
Greenland Proverb

Trees are the most marvellously wonderful natural wonders of Planet Earth. Beautiful magnificent sculptures set within a huge variety of natural landscapes. Trees come in an endless variety of shapes and sizes, forms and textures, some producing colourful leaves, flowers, and fruits. Trees help us connect to the beauty of nature and our surroundings. They are a beautiful symbol of a living organism that creates an ecosystem to provide habitat, shelter, and food for birds and other animals. Trees absorb carbon dioxide and potentially harmful gases from the air and release oxygen into the environment. One large tree can provide a day's supply of oxygen for four people. About half of the human population still uses wood from trees as fuel for cooking and heating. A countless number of items that we use are made out of the bark of trees, such as paper and furniture. At one time man's technology was based on wood. The leaf and bark extract of certain trees have medicinal properties and many studies have shown the therapeutic and healing effects of looking at and being around trees.

Trees can live for over 500 years. In its one lifetime, a tree can filter the air and provide nourishing pure oxygen to millions of creatures. They only draw from the environment that which is essential. We can learn so much from their resilience, strength, and patience through all kinds of weather. They excel most in a community of trees, animals, insects, rocks, soil, and other plants and elements. They nourish themselves with their own fallen leaves. Trees communicate with each other through an underground fungal network and by giving off chemicals above ground, allowing hundreds of trees to behave as a single organism. They support each other by sharing water and nutrients. Trees are our great teacher, wise souls of our beautiful Mother Earth and they deserve our heartfelt respect and admiration. So go ahead, pick a tree and give it your warmest grateful hug.

❋ Start to notice the different kinds of trees around where you live and walk. Go to places in nature where there are trees, notice their size, the shape of the branches, the thickness of the trunk and the shape and colour of the leaves. Look at how the branches and leaves move in the wind. Notice the change in the appearance of trees with the change of the seasons; natural changing sculptures of our environment. Become aware of how the branches themselves look like mini trees. Notice the roots of trees that lay above the ground. How strong they are and how deep they must travel far underneath the ground.

❋ Sit under a tree or near a tree and make friends with it. Contemplate its strengths and beauty. In silence ask it questions, then wait for the responses to come to you. Observe any words or images that come to your mind. Trees can feel our vibrations of love. As trees are connected with each other, sending our vibrations of love to one tree also sends ripples of love to the surrounding trees. Hug or place your hands on a tree, send it your heartfelt love and gratitude.

❋ Become more mindful of all the items around your home, workplace, where you live and travel that are made from trees. How many do you notice? Try and make something yourself from wood. Notice foods that grow on trees, e.g. fruits, vegetables, nuts. While you eat thank the parent tree for providing its food.

❋ Plant a tree. You could plant a seed of a tree or buy a small tree and plant it somewhere special or in memory of someone you love or a special occasion. Plant a tree as your gift to Mother Earth.

❋ Creating art with leaves is a wonderful way of preserving their beauty. Start collecting different sized, shaped, and coloured leaves from all the seasons. Press the leaves in books and create your own leaf art. Make gift cards, or framed art with a meaningful phrase or poem in the centre with leaves surrounding it. Use different parts of trees such as the bark, its seeds, its leaves, even its roots to create works of natural art for your home or garden, be as creative as you like.

❋ See trees as the lungs of the Earth. When outside breathe along with the trees. Your lungs and the Earth's lungs breathing as one.

The Love of Flowers

"If we could see the miracle of a single flower clearly, our whole life would change" The Buddha

Flowers are truly one of nature's most beautiful creations. Their tapestry of bright vibrant colours, lovely scents, and loving nature lifts our hearts when we are around them. We use them to decorate our homes, gardens, bodies and they are used within many traditions and cultures during celebrations and spiritual ceremonies. They symbolise the beauty of nature, peace, wisdom, purity, and innocence.

Flowering plants are thought to have evolved 130 million years ago. There are around half a million species of flowering plants on Earth. They come in all sizes, shapes, forms, and colours. From the tiniest flowers which are the size of a pinhead to the giant rare flowers that grow up to 3 feet tall. Flowers grow amid the harshest conditions of heat and cold, in rainforests, deserts, on mountains, in caves, in the sea, and from mud like the lotus flower.

Without flowering plants, many species including humans would not have evolved on Planet Earth. Flowers are highly adapted to attract their specific pollinators such as bees, flies, moths, hummingbirds, and bats just to name a few. This is why flowers are so brightly coloured and highly scented making them the beautiful creations that they are.

❀ There is great joy to be found in cultivating a flowering plant and watching it grow and flower. Watching flowers bloom throughout the seasons is wonderful; they put a smile on our face and joy in our heart. Try planting a flowering plant from bulb or seed in your garden or in a pot in your home. Nurture and look after it as it grows and flowers. You are showing your gratitude for your flowering plant by helping it bloom. They become a beautiful part of your home, enhancing your life. Many of the flowers that we buy or grow would not exist if it were not for humans cultivating them in mass quantities, we are helping to continue their survival and they return to us the glory of their beauty, stillness, and love.

❀ Take photos of flowers with your mobile phone or camera. Many cameras have flower modes on them to take close-up photos. Capture the beauty of flowers. Many flowers don't live very long, but they bring much joy in their short lives. By taking a photo you are showing your gratitude and extending their life, as each time you look at the photo you continue the love that it's displaying. They make wonderful cards for loved ones.

❀ Make someone special smile by giving them a pot of flowers or a bunch of flowers as a gesture of gratitude. You can either buy the flowers or plant the flower seeds or bulbs yourself, nurture them to start growing and then give these as a gift. It shows you've put your love and effort into growing them. When you give your flowers make a special effort to convey your appreciation and explain why.

♡ Observe the relationship between flowers and insects and how they rely on each other for their survival.

❀ Choose a flower to meditate on. Get a sense of the overall pattern of a flower by scanning its main features. Look deeply at the flower, touch the petals, its stem, drink in its fragrance; observe as much detail as possible. Some petals are exceptionally soft; feel their delicate softness against your skin. It's a lovely experience being kissed by a flower. Become aware of the feelings that arise from your heart when in the presence of the flower. Give the flower your loving presence.

❀ Enjoy the meditative practice of looking after and tending to your flowers. Feel the warmth of love and gratitude from your heart for these precious organisms as you water them, feed them, and protect them. Sense the life-force within these beautiful living things. Enjoy sharing the flowers you take care of with other people.

◌ Offer a flower to something you are grateful for. A beautiful symbol of your love and appreciation.

❀ Create your own flowers using different kinds of art materials and artistic methods. Sketch, paint, mosaic, paper, embroidered, felt, wood, wool, clay. A great way to express your love of flowers. Give a handmade art flower as a gift to someone special.

Sundance

We all love it when the Sun is shining, to feel the warmth on our skin and to see everything around us lit up brightly. The Sun is always there ever-present, whether we can see it or whether it's hidden behind the clouds or at night time when it's on the other side of the Earth.

Without our Sun there would be no life on Earth. It is amazingly the precise distance from the Earth for life to exist. Many cultures and traditions pay respect to the Sun. Ceremonial rituals are performed to honour the Sun. Yoga practitioners salute the Sun with their bodies and in many ancient cultures, the Sun was worshipped as a god. In the northern hemisphere, structures like Stone Henge were built with great effort by people who needed to know where the Sun was in its cycle.

The spectrum of light from the Sun allows us to see all the beautiful array of colours around us. For ancient travellers, the Sun helped to guide the direction of their journey. As the source of energy and life for all living things, the Sun plays a vital role in every function of the mind and body. In humans, it provides essential vitamin D, which is needed for proper immune function, bone growth, strength, and calcium absorption. The light from the Sun also helps to release feel-good happy hormones called endorphins, serotonin, dopamine, and oxytocin into our bodies, which also helps to relieve pain, increase our energy and generate feelings of love. Every plant on Earth needs the Sun's light to produce food and grow; it's the main source of energy for this Planet. The gratitude we need to feel for our glorious Sun is endless.

✏ Take a large piece of paper and draw a Sun in the centre. Make it look bright and colourful using colours of yellow, orange and red. Draw rays coming out of the Sun also in bright colours. Think of the many different ways the Sun helps our Planet and the life form on it. How does the sunshine make you feel? What does the Sun allow you to enjoy? Think of some of your favourite foods and drinks that have been produced by the help of the Sun's energy. Think of as many different ways you are grateful for the Sun and write them down on and at the end of each ray of sunshine.

☺ Being outside in the Sun is beneficial for our health in so many ways, as long as you are using protection from the Sun's strong rays on your skin. The sunshine and warmth from the Sun allow us to do more outdoor activities, increasing our joy and wellbeing. Whenever you are outside enjoying the sunshine, smile and give thanks to the Sun.

☺ When the days are short during the winter, make the most of being outside even in the cold, particularly if you are feeling tired or low, make that special effort to go outside. The light from the Sun will lift your spirits and increase your energy levels, especially as it helps to stimulate and increase feel-good chemicals into the body.

❋ Notice how the colours of the world around you change depending on where the Sun is placed in the sky. When the Sun is high in the sky the colours are bold and strong with dark shadows. During what is known as the golden hour (when the Sun is rising or setting) the colours and textures of what we see around us are much softer. Start to notice how the Sun affects all that you see around you.

⚘ Sit outside in the Sun, on a chair or on the ground, with your eyes closed. Feel the warmth bathing your body. Visualise a warm yellow glow spreading through your body, filling it with healing energies, strengthening you. Give thanks for the vitamin D that is helping to strengthen your bones. This meditation can also be done inside on a cold winter's day. Visualise the Sun's energy beating down on you.

◊ Create your own ritual or ceremony to show your appreciation for the Sun. An ancient ritual called the Sundance was performed every summer by the Native American Indians. Create your own ceremony to show your respect and gratitude to the life-giving Sun.

☺ Every morning just after you've woken up, look through your window, stop for a moment, smile and give thanks for a brand new day. Thank the Sun for lighting your day up.

🌍 Rather than think of the Sun moving across the sky, become aware that it is the Earth spinning around the Sun. Notice how the Earth does its magical dance around the wonderful still Sun.

Moonshine

"It is a beautiful and delightful sight to behold the body of the Moon."
Galileo Galilei

The Moon's beauty and mysterious nature have inspired many writers and lyricists and appeared in many books and songs. Astronomers have studied it and astronauts have explored and walked on its surface. We have all gazed up at the Moon and marvelled at its beauty. On clear nights the Moon shows its beautiful self in its many phases. The Sun's light reflected on its surface as it travels around the Earth. Even when we cannot see its surface during New Moon, it is still there, a constant friend and companion to our dear Earth.

There are many reasons why we should be grateful to our Moon. The Moon is not just a beautiful satellite that circles the Earth; it has played a vital role in the formation of life on Earth; without it, we would not be here. The Moon has an incredible gravitational pull on the Earth, generating something called the tidal force. Millions of years ago the Moon was closer to the Earth, creating very high tides and low tides on the Earth's water. This whirlpool effect is thought to have helped life to form in the oceans. The Moon also stabilises our Earth by its gravitational pull, allowing the Earth to revolve at the right speed on its axis.

It's quite extraordinary how the surface of the Moon exactly covers the surface of the Sun during a total eclipse of the Sun. There seems to be a special unique connection between the Moon, Earth, and Sun. Their distances away from each other have perfectly allowed life to exist on Planet Earth.

✡ On days when you can see the Moon in its many phases, send it your gratefulness. Thank the Moon for helping to create life on Earth and for being part of giving you the life that you have. Make the Moon your friend and share with it through your heart what you are grateful for. You could pray, meditate or ask questions to the Moon through your mind and heart.

✡ Look up at the Moon and send it a message of love, healing or gratitude for someone, something, a group of people or a particular place that you care about. Transmit your positive vibrations to the Moon and it will shine your message back over the Planet.

✡ If you have binoculars or a telescope, you will be able to see all the incredible craters on the Moon. The Moon is about a quarter of the size of the Earth, so these craters are very large indeed. Looking up it is hard not to marvel at the sheer beauty of the Moon and its craters.

✡ Many cultures use a lunar calendar based on the cycles of the Moon's phases. The Moon plays a significant part in cultural festivals. Many harvest festivals around the world are held on full Moon days during the year. The Moon Festival is an important celebration in many Asian and tribal cultures and many ceremonies take place during the new Moon, such as Hindu and Chinese New Year's Day. Find out when the cultural festivals relating to the Moon are and their meaning. Perhaps in some way you can join in with these festivals and show your gratitude in your own way for what is being celebrated.

✡ From a source such as the internet or a book, find out all the New Moon days and Full Moon days of the year. Make a note on your calendar or diary or mobile phone of these days. There is one New Moon and one Full Moon within approximately 28 days. Generally, a Full Moon will appear around 14 days after the New Moon. On each Full Moon day decide to practice gratitude of some kind. Keep the same practice until the next New Moon, so for about 14 days, you will enhance a particular practice of gratitude. Then on the New Moon, you start again with another practice of gratitude of your choice, choosing a different focus and emphasis throughout each phase. You can choose from any of the practices in this book or you can invent your own. Focusing on a particular gratitude practice for many days in a row increases your awareness and helps to gradually change the way you perceive things, eventually creating a positive change in your way of being.

✡ Do a Moonwalking meditation. Either with eyes closed or using an image of the Moon's surface in front of you imagine you are wearing a spacesuit and walking on the Moon. Imagine each mindful step.

Journey Creation of the Stars

"Of all things visible, the highest is the heaven of the fixed stars."
Nicolaus Copernicus

When our lovely Sun has set for the day, other Suns which are many light years away come out to show their bright and beautiful light; we call them stars, and they fill our night sky with their brilliant points of light. We know that our Father Sun has helped create and sustain life on Earth, but do we think about all the other stars in the universe and what part they have played in creating life in the world around us?

Science has shown that most of the material on our Planet, including ourselves, is made from stardust, from an exploding star. So we can easily say that the stars are our ancestors. Almost every atom in our body was made inside a star, we are the children of stardust, it's a lovely thought.

When we look up at the stars, we cannot even comprehend how far they are away from us. The light that has reached our eyes from these stars had left the stars hundreds, thousands or millions of years ago. The stars are teaching us our history, lighting our awareness, silently showing us our ancestral lineage.

It's nice to be aware that the light from these stars must have been seen by all the generations of people before us and will be seen by all the generations of people after us. The light from all the stars is never-ending and we are very fortunate to be able to witness their brightness and to look up at them with great respect and awe.

There are about 100 billion galaxies in the observable universe. The number of stars in a galaxy varies, but assuming an average of 100 billion stars per galaxy means that there are about 1 billion trillion stars in the observable universe. Our minds, hearts, spirits cannot help expanding greatly with this awareness. Each star out there is a Sun; many of them may have Planets revolving around it. Imagine how many Planets there must be, all different, with a great possibility of life on them.

✡ On a clear night, lie down on your back outside and look up at the dark expansive night sky. As you gaze, open your heart to the immensities of the cosmos. Become aware of the countless stars you can see, let your eyes adjust slowly to the darkness. Feel grateful to night time when the skies open up a beautiful magical display of twinkling stars. Feel part of the great expansive universe that we live in.

✡ Learn some of the names of the stars, start to familiarise yourself with them and the constellations. Maybe use binoculars or a telescope to get a closer look at the stars or even one of the Planets in the solar system. Once you start becoming more aware of the stars or planets in the night sky, you'll start to look up naturally every time you are out in the dark and begin to appreciate their wonder and the infinite vastness of the universe.

✡ See yourself as made of stardust, when you look up at a star, feel the connection between you and the star. Perhaps you'd like to choose a particular star and learn more about it. You can then look out for it and form a deeper connection with it, like adopting it as a brother or sister. After all, you are related in some way to every star.

✡ Look out for shooting stars (meteors) as they fly over the night sky. If you go to a very dark place, where there is no light pollution, you may see the Milky Way galaxy; billions of stars stretching out across the sky.

✡ Find an ultra-deep field image online. If you hold a pin at arm's length in the air, the head of the pin covers approximately the amount of sky that appears in this image. Every point of light is a galaxy, around 10,000 in this image. Absolutely incredible!

✡ If you could communicate with an alien from another planet what one question would you ask it?

✡ In meditation create your own planet. What kind of life is on it, how do the creatures live, how do they communicate? What do the landscapes look like? See where your imagination takes you. Grateful for the diversity of life that must surely exist out there in the universe.

Breathe My Dear

"When the breath is irregular, the mind is also unsteady; but when the breath is still, so is the mind." Hathayogapradipika

Every breath we take keeps us alive. Oxygen is the most vital nutrient for our bodies. The Earth's atmosphere provides us with fresh clean air, free-of-charge. Our lungs take in the air from the atmosphere through the nose and mouth and along with the heart transports the oxygen in the air to the brain and to all the cells and organs of our body so that they can function efficiently and keep us alive. Our lungs then release waste products such as carbon dioxide and toxins back into the atmosphere. With a normal sedentary way of living, we only use about 10 percent of our total lung capacity. Incorrect shallow breathing due to stress, anxiety, unhealthy habits or tight clothing results in a lack of oxygen to our brain and body which can then create tension in our heads and affects all our organs, muscles and joints.

Breathing exercises are a very important part of yoga practice, synchronising body movements with the in-breath and out-breath, helping to connect to and enhance life force. Full abdominal breathing lowers the diaphragm and expands the ribcage allowing more oxygen into the lungs, therefore increasing the oxygen into all our cells. The many benefits of this increased oxygen intake are improved energy levels, better digestive function, improved immune function, increased circulation, rejuvenated nervous system, relaxed muscles, lower stress levels, balanced hormones, and increased efficiency of brain function.

Breathing is also an important part of many meditation practices, particularly in Buddhist meditations, tai-chi, and many martial arts. Our natural conscious breath is used as an amazing tool to concentrate and unite the mind and body, allowing the mind to become still and centred, bringing the energy of mindfulness into each moment. Each breath is a bridge between the mind and the body.

☺ In meditation, choose a particular part of your body, perhaps an area that needs your attention. Slowly, mindfully imagine your natural breath travelling in and out of this area, nourishing and healing every part of it.

☺ Mindful natural breath meditation – Close your eyes and bring your attention to your natural in-breath and out-breath. Feel the natural flow of air coming in and out of your nose. Feel how the abdomen and chest rises and falls with each breath. Concentrate your mind on the sensations from your nose as you breathe in and out. If you become carried away by your thoughts, your worries, your emotions, and perceptions, your breath gently anchors your mind back into the present moment like a faithful friend who helps you come back to your true self. Notice how calm, light and peaceful your breathing becomes when you are still and mindful, like a gentle wave. Notice how the breath takes attention away from your thinking and creates space inside your mind, body, and spirit. Enjoy every breath. Feel the miracle of how the body naturally allows air to flow in and out, nourishing and giving you the gift of life in every single moment. Each mindful breath is a meditation.

☺ Take a few deep breaths when you are outside in the fresh air. Feel grateful for this glorious free air that keeps you alive, drink it into your body. Be thankful for the Earth's atmosphere, for the abundance of oxygen around you and the joy of breathing it into your body. Take three deep conscious breaths at any time to centre yourself into the present.

☺ Mindful deep abdominal breathing – You can do this practice with one hand placed on your abdomen and the other hand placed on your chest in a seated, standing or lying down position. To fully use your lungs, breathe deeply, slowly and fully in this sequence being mindful of the movement of the air through different parts of the body. Breathe in through your nose into your abdomen; feel your stomach rise first as the diaphragm pushes down upon it. The air then travels up to your chest; feel your lungs expand. Next, feel the air in the upper chest near your collarbone. The breath then reaches your throat, then finally your nose. Hold the air inside your body for a count of 5. When releasing the air, release from your nose, throat, collarbone, then your chest, then finally your abdomen. Follow the movement of your breath out of these areas in your body. Regular practice of deep abdominal breathing trains the body to naturally take in more oxygen. This kind of breathing shuts off the stress response, switches on the healing response and can calm the mind instantly. This practice can be done anywhere at any time with hands placed on your stomach and chest or without.

Nutritional Blessings

"Let food be thy medicine and medicine be thy food." Hippocrates

Food is a basic human need. It provides vital fuel and essential nutrients such as protein, fats, carbohydrates, vitamins and minerals for us to stay alive; feeding all our cells, tissues and organs which make up our body. For those of us who are readily provided with food on a daily basis, it's easy to take the food we eat for granted.

Around 800 million people continue to struggle with hunger every day, that's about one in ten people on Earth. 1.2 billion people still live in extreme poverty. Each year, 2.6 million children die as a result of hunger-related causes. Knowing these facts we really need to be grateful for every bit of food that we receive, at the same time understanding that overconsumption of food can damage our health and that a balanced eating pattern is important. When we consider that so many people go hungry every day, we need to be more mindful of not wasting the food that is given to us. Because food is so readily available in our society, people tend to overbuy food; consequently, so much food goes to waste and is thrown away. An estimated 1.3 billion tonnes of food or roughly 30 percent of global production is lost or wasted annually. It is important for us to become grateful and more aware of the food we eat and consume, and do what we can to help those who struggle with hunger.

🍎 Be a smart, conscientious shopper and consumer. Think about the food you are buying and when it will be eaten. Wasting food is often a habit. Become aware of how much food you throw away, request smaller portions, plan meals and use shopping lists. Bring your leftovers home from restaurants in reusable containers, donate food to food banks, and pack up leftover food for your friends and family to take away. In this way, you will save food, save money and help protect the environment.

🍎 Make a nice meal to show someone how grateful you are to them or take them out for a nice meal. Feeding someone is one of the best gifts you can give as it is nourishing and is gratefully received.

🍎 Give thanks before you eat your meals and while eating. Take a moment to pause to look at the food you are about to eat. Recognise the many factors involved and all the people who took time and effort to feed and nourish you, whose hard work was necessary for you to have food on your table. Each time you eat, allow images to pop into your mind relating to the meal you are eating, such as a particular food item in its whole state, where and how some of the food is grown, how it was produced, the people who may have been involved, the cooks, the farmers, the crops, the grocery store, the machinery, processes, and transport involved, the elements such as the Sun, clouds, rain, compost, and pollinators. Choose a particular item in your meal and see where your mind takes you. Send your grateful thoughts and feelings to all these elements as well as feeling blessed that you have all of the food and nourishment you need to live a healthy life.

🍎 Foodbanks distribute food to those who have difficulty purchasing enough to avoid hunger. Donate food to your local foodbank or host a collection at your school, local group, and workplace or amongst family and friends.

🍎 Raise money for food aid charities by taking part in sponsored challenges or making and selling food. Be creative in how you can raise funds to help people who are struggling with hunger and at the same time educate others and raise awareness of the situation the world is facing regarding food shortages and wastage.

🍎 Research a certain food you eat and learn more about it. How does it grow, where does it come from and what are its benefits to your body and health. Share what you've learned with others. Try out foods you've never eaten. Be grateful for the wonderful nutrients the food is giving you and the strength the food gives you. While you are eating visualise the nutrients of the food entering your cells, nourishing your body. Be mindful that the food you eat becomes part of you and contains the building blocks for your whole body. Involve your senses while you are cooking and eating. Appreciate how the food looks, the smell, touch, and taste of food. Try out new recipes from books, friends, TV shows and the internet. Give yourself enough time and enjoy the process of cooking and eating.

Our Immune System Friends

The immune system is a marvellous complex network of cells, tissues, and organs that work together to help protect and defend the body from harmful organisms and substances that can cause disease. Our immune system friends work tirelessly day and night to protect the body. They are our internal warriors, constantly on the lookout for foreign particles. We need to appreciate and look after our immune system friends for them to respect and look after us in return. If we constantly put stress on the mind, body and spirit, the immune system will become drained and weak, compromising its ability to protect us efficiently. So let us increase our gratitude, love, and respect for the immune system, and also understand and listen to what it's trying to tell us when we become ill.

☺ Everyone has some stress; it's part of life, but if stress drags on for a long time, it makes us more vulnerable to illness, from colds and infections to serious diseases. Chronic stress exposes the body to a steady stream of stress hormones that suppress the immune system and can eventually through prolonged stress cause it to attack our own cells. Find the best ways to manage stress to help bring your body back to balance. Listen to your body. Are you feeling overly tired, run-down, stressed and are getting colds or ill regularly? Then it's time to slow down, look at ways of changing your lifestyle and dealing with the stressful conditions of your life. Do activities that you enjoy and lift your spirits. Rest and relax your mind and body regularly. Speak and feel kindly and compassionately towards yourself. Learn about meditation and mindfulness techniques. Find a practice that suits you the best. Studies have shown that people who meditate regularly have healthier immune system responses.

☺ Having strong relationships and a good social network is good for you. People who feel connected to friends whether it's a few close friends or a large group have stronger immunity. Thinking and feeling positive is very important to your health and wellbeing. Practising gratitude in its various forms naturally increases our positivity and makes us feel more connected to the people and the world around us.

☺ Research has shown that practising gratitude increases the release of Immunoglobulin A (IgA), an antibody which boosts the immune system function. Just 10 minutes of gratitude practice per day increases IgA by 50% and by an amazing 140% if practiced while listening to music that inspires, uplifts, relaxes; music that you love.

☺ What we eat plays a very important role in helping our immune system friends. Green and brightly coloured fruits and vegetables are rich in immune-boosting properties, so make sure your meals are as colourful as possible. Garlic and ginger also help fight viruses and bacteria. Spices love to help the immune system especially the colourful orange spice turmeric. Research the foods and drinks that help nourish your immune system and try to slowly include them in your daily meals.

☺ Gentle, moderate exercise such as walking for 30 minutes a day helps to boost the body's feel-good chemicals from the brain and also helps you sleep better, both good for the immune system.

☺ They say that laughter is the best medicine. We feel great when we have a good laugh. Laughter curbs the levels of stress hormones in our body and boosts a type of white blood cell that fights infection. Just anticipating a funny event can have a positive effect on our immune system. So go ahead and feed your immune system friends with a good laugh.

☺ If you are ill, you can help your immune system by visualising your immune cell friends inside your body as they spread to the areas where they are needed the most. Visualise the immune cells surrounding, flooding and embracing the areas which need healing. Your immune cells could be colourful balls of happy faces gobbling up the harmful cells, or you could imagine the immune system as a wave of white or golden light travelling and dissolving harmful invaders. Visualise your immune cells as anything you like; spaceships, bubbles, animals, swimming sea creatures, perhaps invent a story involving many different characters, let your imagination go wild and be as creative as you like. You can do an immune system boosting visualisation at any time. Talk to your immune system and send it lots of love.

The Wellness of Illness

"One can cause the illness which he wanted to cure." Kikuyu Proverb

Illness, whether it be physical or mental, is a natural part of life. We have all suffered from some kind of illness. Illnesses which are short-lived or illnesses which have lasted longer. If we look deeply, some illnesses have a benefit. Some illnesses help to build and strengthen our immune system. Illness and pain are signs for us to rest and allows us to take notice and be more mindful of our body, mind, and health. Illness is a clear message from our body to stop and take notice. It allows us to learn ways to find balance in our lives.

Within every form of illness, there is something that it is trying to tell us. Rather than fight with an illness, we must embrace and understand what it is trying to teach us; what it wants for us to learn and what it's guiding us to do and the person it wants us to become. Illness teaches us to be more grateful for the gift of life that we have been given. Illness forces us to see which areas in our life need balancing. It teaches us to respect our body and mind. It pushes us to learn more about ourselves, what the mind and body really needs to heal. Illness can change our perception of how we see the world around us. It can close certain doors and open up new opportunities; it can help change our life for the better. We can transform an illness into something positive; it helps us understand others who suffer from the same kind of illness or any kind of illness. If we have overcome a great challenge with illness or are learning to live with the illness we can carry on to help others with their health challenges.

☺ Mental, physical or emotional discomfort or pain is our body speaking to us in its own unique language. Sometimes it gives us small niggling hints, sometimes it's a soft voice that comes and goes and sometimes it is a full-blown cry for help. Mindful awareness and gratitude for our body help us to tune in and take notice of it. What is your body saying to you right now? Investigate steps you can take to help nurture your mind and body to a healthier happier balanced place. There are plenty of resources available to help re-balance our mind and body.

☺ There is so much gratefulness we can feel for those who look after us while we are ill and those who have helped us throughout our illness. We can be grateful for our family and friends who have helped us and cared for us during our illness. Grateful for all the people in the medical profession who help us – doctors, nurses, carers, all those who were responsible for producing the medication, natural or conventional, that help us heal or relieve us of pain. Thank all the people and factors that are involved in bringing the medication into our lives and all the healthcare teachers. Think of all the people involved in taking care of your health, feel grateful for the huge part they played in supporting you in your recovery and comfort.

☺ Look back at when you were ill, whatever the illness was, and feel grateful for having the illness and how you came through it all and are now healthier. Remember all the things you did to make yourself better and the people who helped you. What did you learn from the whole experience? How has it changed you? How has it changed your perceptions of your body and mind, of life in general? What did you learn about yourself, has it taught you ways to take more care of yourself, how has it taught you to help others? Be thankful for your illness. If you are suffering now with an illness or have been for a long time, do the same exercise, look at all the ways in which your illness is helping you, feel and show your gratitude to those who are helping you. How has it made you more deeply understand others who have an illness? Anything that happens to us has its purpose, although we may not see it at the time, if we look deeply enough we will see its benefit. Something beautiful will always come out of this journey and we will always learn something beneficial from our great teacher illness. Think of an illness as a great opportunity to learn ways to heal your mind, body, and spirit.

☺ Learn from those who have used their illness or disability to help others and achieve great things in spite of their condition. Learn from people who have overcome an illness of some kind. There are now countless true stories of people who have used a variety of natural methods to cure themselves of serious to life-threatening illnesses. Do some research and become inspired by their passion to heal themselves.

A Good Night's Sleep

"Day full-blown and splendid-day of the immense Sun, action, ambition, laughter. The Night follows close with millions of Suns, and sleep and restoring darkness." Walt Whitman

Sleep is essential to a person's health and wellbeing as it is involved in healing and repair of the heart and blood vessels and plays a critical role in immune function, metabolism, memory, learning, and other vital functions. With all these benefits it's no wonder we feel so great after getting a good night's sleep, but it's the quality of sleep rather than the number of hours' sleep that's important.

Stress, tension, anxiety, fear, worry, loneliness, emotional and physical pain, keeping our minds too active and not being able to wind down all prevent us from getting good sleep.

Practising gratitude during your day and before you go to sleep will greatly improve your state of mind, helping you to see yourself and the world around you in a positive way. Gratitude helps improve your relationships and enhances present moment awareness. This general appreciation of life will help you sleep so much better. The better sleep you get the healthier in mind and body you will feel and subsequently you will be better able to deal with challenges that may come your way.

🧘 Doing meditation can take us into a sleepy brainwave state. Beta brainwave is when we are in the alert waking state. Alpha brainwave state is when we are in deep relaxation. Theta is a brainwave state when we are drifting off to sleep and Delta is when we are in deep sleep. Listening to a guided meditation or do your own meditation before you go to bed or while lying in bed can take you from Beta into Alpha, then Theta and finally into Delta for a wonderful night's sleep.

✏ Every night before you go to sleep, write down something you a grateful for in a journal. Before you go to sleep, share something you are grateful for or something you were grateful for during the day with someone you live with or on the phone with someone close. You could both make the habit of doing this practice every night before you go to sleep. Your waking mind closes the day and starts its restful sleep with a deeply felt positive thought.

🧘 We lie down to sleep for about a third of our life. What we lie on is a wonderfully comfortable bed with a soft pillow to cushion our head and a warm blanket to keep our body warm. Think about the many people in the world who do not have a bed to sleep on, the many homeless and those who live in poverty. We should be so grateful that we have a comfortable place to lay our body and great respect for the bed we sleep on. Every time you get into bed and lie down, be grateful for your bed. Every time you wake up in the morning, be grateful for your bed. You can make an extra effort in the morning by making sure your bed is nice and tidy, your pillow and blanket in place. Every time you change the bedcovers, sheets and pillow covers again give your bed that extra attention and send it your thoughts and feelings of gratitude.

🧘 Do the 3-phase grateful bedtime sleeping meditation.

Phase 1 – Before you get into bed, before you go to sleep, give thanks for the day that has just passed, for everything that you have learned and experienced.

Phase 2 – While in bed, thank your cosy bed, give thanks for the rest and sleep you are about to have.

Phase 3 – When you wake up the next morning give thanks for the sleep and rest that you have had for the past several hours and give thanks for the new day that you are about to experience.

In this way you are feeling appreciation for the life you have been given and the bed that supports you in the transition from your busy day into a restful night and from your relaxed sleep into another grateful day.

The Beauty of a Smile

"For me, every hour is grace. And I feel gratitude in my heart each time I can meet someone and look at his or her smile." Elie Wiesel

A smile is a wonderful expression of our kindness, joy, and happiness. We all smile for many different reasons. We smile when we find something amusing or humorous or when we are feeling joyful or silly. We smile when we are greeting someone or when we are happy to see someone or something. We smile when we are inwardly content or when we are showing kindness. We smile to ourselves as an expression of our inner joy. We even smile as a way to hide our nervousness and also help lighten the nervousness within ourselves and sometimes we smile to put someone at ease. A smile can be a slight turning up of the corners of the mouth to a full-blown toothy grin. Our eyes along with our mouth express our smile. Our whole face lights up to express our inner joy and the beauty of our spirit. A smile can be contagious; it can spread; when you smile at someone they will most likely smile back at you.

To be able to express our feelings through our smile, to see someone else smile, to share our smile and pass it onto others and to have this outward expression of our inward beauty is something to be very grateful for. A smile affects other people's attitudes and behaviours. A smile for someone can improve their mood which then has a positive effect on those that they come into contact with during the day. The positive energy of your smile has a ripple effect, its wavelike energy continues on to others.

☺ Try to smile more throughout the day. When you meet someone, show them your smile, show how happy you are to see them, share your inner spirit with them; this shows them that you are a friendly soul and they will feel more comfortable in your presence and lighter in spirit. You may receive a smile from them in return but if not then you would have certainly lit up their inner smile. Just as a lit candle can light another candle, a smile can light a smile within another person's face and heart.

☺ Compliment someone on their smile. Take photos of smiles.

☺ We get to see our own smile when we see a photograph of ourselves smiling. How much better we look when we smile, our face just glows and we look happier. When you are in front of a mirror on your own, look at your face, think of something nice and smile to yourself. See your own face smiling back at you. Look at how your face is transformed. This is the lovely smiling face that others see when you smile at them. Seeing your face smiling back at you brings out the feelings of joy that are always sitting within you. Feel grateful for the inner and outer expression of your smile.

☺ When you are around people look at their faces, become observant and look for their smiles. Their smiles could be very subtle or they could be big and bright. See how many smiles you notice in a day. How does noticing other people's smiles make you feel? Notice your own inner and outer smile slowly immerging during this practice.

☺ Studies have shown that smiling can improve your mood and reduce stress. A full smile that involves facial muscles around the eyes and muscles around the mouth sends a feedback message to the brain which triggers the release of feel-good happy healing chemicals into the brain, helping to reduce stress and increase feelings of happiness. So go ahead and put a smile on your face now and feel what happens.

☺ In meditation recall memories of people you know smiling. Think of someone now; remember their smile and smile with them. In meditation imagine the shared smiles filling the space.

☺ When you are fearful or angry or sad, smile at your fear, anger, sadness, and say "hello my fear, anger or sadness". Placing your mindful smiling presence on the emotion will help lighten the feeling.

☺ Working in a group or on your own, cut out paper or card circles. Draw a smiling face on one side of the circle, using different coloured pens, pencils or paints. On the other side of the circle write your own grateful message. The smiling face messages can be hung up somewhere or given as a gift to someone special.

Laughter is the Best Medicine

"I've decided to be happy because it is good for my health." Voltaire

Laughter is one of the best ways to lighten the mind. It makes us feel instantly better and provides long-term health benefits. The positive feelings of laughter have many stress-relieving effects as it helps to release endorphins from the brain, which are natural painkillers, and helps to relieve symptoms of stress. Laughter improves the immune system, enhances the intake of oxygen-rich air and stimulates the heart, lungs, and muscles. It's like having an internal workout.

Laughter certainly is the best medicine and completely free. It helps us connect with other people and it also helps us cope with difficult situations. There are so many benefits to having a good laugh. Laughter is used as a therapy in many countries to bring people together, to help lighten the mind, reduce stress levels and improve health.

In the true story *'Anatomy of an Illness'*, Norman Cousins writes how he used laughter to help relieve his pain from a life-threatening illness. He found that two hours of 'belly laughter', watching funny films allowed him two hours of pain-free sleep. His amazing survival story inspired much research into the effects of laughter and positive emotions on health.

☺ Laughter is contagious. Have you ever noticed when others are laughing around us, we laugh along with them? The laughter and joy of others is infectious; just listening to someone laugh is funny. Funny comedy films are a wonderful way of generating laughter. From time to time, watch films that will make you laugh; watch them with your family and friends, laugh together and feel grateful for enjoying this wonderful experience together. Feel grateful for all the people involved in making the funny film, grateful to be sharing this laughter with those around you, grateful for the laughter that makes you feel so much better and helps improve your health and grateful that you are blessed with this ability of your mind and body to produce a spontaneous act of physical joy.

☺ Together with family and friends recall moments from the past that made you laugh, remember those moments and bring back the essence of the laughter you experienced in the past into the present moment. Look back and laugh about funny experiences from the past or even when you laughed so much that it was unbearable. We can always remember a time in our life when we laughed so much it brought tears to our eyes or laughed so much that our belly ached; these are truly unforgettable moments of pure joy.

☺ Do something silly, spontaneous, something out of the ordinary that would make you and others laugh. Do some karaoke, dance in a silly manner, wear some outrageous clothes, tell a joke.

☺ Going to live comedy plays and shows or routines encourages laughter amongst a large group of people. It's great to share laughter with so many people in one space. A collective energy of laughter creates a surge of positive emotions amongst everyone in the room.

☺ Try not to take life too seriously and laugh at yourself about things that don't go as expected. Try and see the funny side of life. Think back to a time where something went wrong, it didn't go as planned. Can you now laugh about it? Turn it into a humorous story and tell others about it. Lighten the whole story and laugh together about the absurdness of the situation.

☺ Watch and listen to people while they are laughing. Notice the change in their facial expressions and the movements of their body. Feel the positive vibrations flowing out of them. If you are laughing, become aware of your physical expressions, and elevated emotions. How do you feel after you've had a good laugh?

☺ Laughter yoga is a practice involving prolonged voluntary laughter based on the belief that voluntary laughing provides the same physiological and psychological benefits as spontaneous laughter. Laughter yoga is done in groups, with jokes and playfulness between participants. Find a laughter yoga class near you and try it out.

Life's Simple Pleasures

"There are two ways to live: you can live as if nothing is a miracle, or you can live as if everything is a miracle." Albert Einstein

They say "the best things in life are free" or "it's always the little things". Life is filled with simple pleasures, the little satisfying effects we take great pleasure in. They are the gifts of life that we each celebrate in our own unique way. A perfect day does not have to be extraordinary. Life's simple pleasures are often the greatest pleasures.

We have to learn to savour life, to actively look for the joy waiting to be found in life. When we discover how to do this, it's like we are looking at the world through fresh eyes, through another lens. Without having to spend a lot of money, we get to have a richer life simply through a change of perspective.

These simple pleasures pop up throughout our day. They're not big things, but each simple pleasure can translate to a great day if you acknowledge and feel grateful for them. Value the simple moments in your day, as if they were gifts given to you. So set a goal today to slow down enough to savour the simple things in your day today; to look for the wonder waiting to be found in the ordinary elements that make up your day.

☺ Make a list of your favourite simple pleasures. What brings a smile onto your face and a warm uplifting feeling within your heart?

☺ When you become aware of a simple pleasure, slow down and really savour the moment. Acknowledge that this is a wonderful moment and feel grateful for receiving it. Allow this feeling to stay with you throughout your day and share how you felt about it to someone else, encouraging them to enjoy their own unique simple pleasures. Ask someone to share which moments they savoured in their day. Finding thankfulness for all of life's simple pleasures regardless of circumstance generates joy and makes us feel truly alive.

Here are some examples of simple pleasures to give you some ideas and to spark other ideas of your own.

- Listening to your favourite music in the car
- A relaxing shower or bath
- A stunning sunset
- Bringing a smile to someone's face
- Flowers beginning to bloom on a spring day
- Receiving an unexpected compliment
- Watching children giggle and play
- The first sip of a beverage when you are thirsty
- Receiving a card, letter or a package
- Reading a book that resonates with you
- Listening to birds singing
- Enjoying a home-cooked meal with your family
- Reminiscing about old times with a friend
- A long walk
- Freshly baked bread
- Helping someone in need
- Having a picnic
- Enjoying your favourite exercise activity
- A warm hug
- Having a good laugh
- Breathing in fresh air
- Climbing into bed with freshly washed sheets
- Watching animals in nature
- Freshly squeezed fruit juice
- Lying back and looking up at the clouds or stars
- Watching an old movie
- A nice warm drink

These moments of simple pleasures are endless, each of us experiencing and feeling the joys of being alive in our own unique way. Start to notice these pleasures more and more throughout your day. Feel grateful for all the special gifts and treats of life's simple pleasures you receive, as if every day were your birthday or a day of celebration.

Language of the Skies

"Sunshine is delicious, rain is refreshing, wind braces us up, snow is exhilarating; there is really no such thing as bad weather, only different kinds of good weather." John Ruskin

The state of the atmosphere around us changes from moment to moment and from season to season depending on where we are in the world. The weather is the language of the skies, expressing itself in its many different ways. A glorious dance with the clouds, with the temperature, with the movement of the Earth around the Sun. All of life on Earth has a beautiful and special relationship with the weather. We can be influenced on many levels by how the weather wishes to express itself. We all react to it in our many different ways, either positive or negative, all depending on what we wish to do, how we feel, what we are wearing, where we are situated in relation to it and our previous experiences of it. The weather is something we have no control over at all, so why not embrace whatever it is trying to express. Welcome the weather each day, each moment with acceptance and appreciation; making sure you protect yourself if the weather is too harsh.

🌍 Form a more mindful healthier relationship with the weather. Whichever season you are in and whatever the weather may be, if the weather in your mind is good or bad, or whatever mood you may be in, first realise that you have absolutely no control over it. Knowing this fact you wish to embrace the weather in the way it chooses to express itself in that moment. In your heart and mind, look for the beauty within it. Whether it's sunny, raining, snowing, windy, cloudy, grey or bright, look at the beauty in it, feel the wonder of it. Use all your senses to understand the weather. Use all your senses to pick up on the subtle nuances of the weather, allow the Earth's atmosphere to communicate with you. Feel what it is saying to you and respond back with your gratitude for this beautiful relationship.

🌍 Look up the sky, if there are clouds, watch what they are doing, how they are dancing and expressing themselves in the wide landscape of the skies. Are the clouds moving? If so, watch how they move and change shape. Do the shapes of the clouds remind you of anything you can be grateful for? If the clouds are dark and grey, find the beauty within the vast expansive dark skies and its reflection over the landscapes.

🌍 The snow can invite many different feelings within us, as does all types of weather, but why not enjoy it when it arrives. Make snowmen, go sledging, go walking in the countryside. Freshly fallen snow can look so beautiful like the whole landscape has been cleaned to a brilliant white, freshly new. Feel the wonder of the snow, watch its snowflakes fall so delicately over the landscape.

🌍 The wind has many different subtle forms. It invites a breath of fresh air. We embrace a soft breeze, especially on a hot day. Some winds are so strong and powerful, they have a stunning beauty of their own. We see the wind in the way it moves nature around us, through the trees and landscape, along the many forms of water on Earth. We can feel its language on our skin when we are in touch with it. It can be soft and warm or sharp, refreshing and cold. Start to become mindful of how the wind feels upon your skin and as you breathe it in through your nose and into your body. Listen to the sound of the wind, grateful as you embrace all its subtle voices.

🌍 When you notice a negative remark about the weather, whether you have said it or someone else has, turn it around to a positive statement. Change your attitude in the moment and express a refreshingly alternative view of the glorious weather. When it's a pleasant day weather-wise we sometimes say to ourselves or others what a lovely day it is, which helps lift our mood. Start to practice saying "What a lovely day it is" to yourself or when you meet people, whatever the weather may be like. It may be raining, or snowing, windy, very cold, too hot, cloudy and grey, it's always a lovely day weather-wise. When describing the weather, use positive and creative words to reflect on how you feel about it. Words such as refreshing, glorious, warming, cosy, exhilarating, festive, crisp, tropical, wonderful, nourishing. Turn a normally unpleasant view of the weather to something refreshingly different, especially when engaged in conversation with someone else. Your positive attitude will hopefully filter into someone else's mind and heart, helping to change their view of the weather.

Raindance

◆ Look up and appreciate the clouds. Watch how they float by or hang there like majestic sculptures in the sky. They form so many wonderful shapes. Choose a cloud – what does it look most like to you? Looking up at the cloud, the great water carrier, express your warm gratitude to it for providing you and the Earth with its water. It's like the clouds are blessing you and the Earth with its drops of water.

◆ Cultures from ancient Egypt and Native American tribes performed a Raindance to invoke rain. Do a visualised rain meditation to recorded rain sounds. Imagining yourself dancing in the rain or any other scene involving the rain. Generate the sensations of the rain on your body.

◆ On a rainy day find a sheltered place outside in which to sit or sit inside with the window open. Close your eyes and take a few deep breathes to ground yourself. As you become more present tune into the natural sounds around you. The splashing of the rain in puddles, the rustling of the wet leaves, the singing of the birds, the distance rush of cars on wet roads. Become aware of your feelings about the rain at that moment. Then start to really look at the rain, watch it fall and look at where it falls. If it is falling on buildings and cars, think of it as washing the buildings and cars clean, as if they are having a shower. If the rain is falling on trees and plants think of it nourishing them, giving them a great nutritious drink and helping them grow and be healthy. Close your eyes and listen to the rain as it falls. The sound can be wonderful and soothing. Imagine your mind and whole body getting an internal shower, feeling cleansed and refreshed.

◆ When you find yourself in a conversation regarding the rain, and it's tending towards the negative, turn it around and talk about the many benefits of rain. Other people will be pleasantly surprised by your positive outlook, allowing them to see the rain differently.

◆ Next time you drink something, see a cloud floating in your drink.

◆ Place your palm face up or turn your face upwards and feel the rain as it touches your hand and face. Get in touch with the rain.

A Voyage of Discovery

"The real voyage of discovery consists not in seeking new landscapes, but in having new eyes." Marcel Proust

Remember how it was when you experienced something for the very first time, how your senses were heightened, how it made you feel. Even though you may have experienced something several times during your life, try to experience something as if it were absolutely your very first time ever. It's a wonderful meditation that can dramatically enhance your moment-to-moment experience.

👁 It may help to imagine that your consciousness has arrived into your body for the first time and that everything is new to you or even that you are an alien from another Planet experiencing things of this Planet for the first time. You can also imagine you have a child's mind, a mind of wonder, curiosity, and amazement as you experience something.

Choose something that you'd like to do this meditation on, such as walking for the first time, breathing for the first time, taking a shower for the first time, eating for the first time, getting a hug for the first time, seeing a flower or a tree for the first time, hearing bird song for the first time, any experience at all. Engage all your senses; sight, sounds, smells, touch and taste as if you are experiencing them for the first time also. Engage your heart, what are your moment-to-moment feelings with each sensation. It's truly an all-encompassing experience, enhancing our awareness to a far greater quality, allowing us to become very deeply connected to the present moment and increasing our feelings of gratitude for each moment during the experience; increasing our feelings of wonder and awe. You can do the same practice listening to music or hearing information for the first time. Even though you may have heard it several times in your life, purposely experience it for the first time. Choose something to practice on now, slip a brand new mind into your brand new body, transporting yourself into a brand new world, a wonderful voyage of discovery.

Anything is Possible

"Start by doing what's necessary; then do what's possible; and suddenly you are doing the impossible." St Francis of Assisi

Sometimes things don't go as planned and mistakes are made, you put so much effort into something and it didn't work out. Don't give up, be grateful for what you have learned from the experience, pick yourself up and try again. Next time around you may choose to do things differently, your perspective will have changed from the last experience and this only adds a wiser quality to every experience that follows. Believe in yourself, and the rest will fall into place. Have faith in your abilities; anything is possible.

⚘ Think back to a time when something you tried, worked for, hoped for, didn't happen the first time around and maybe a few more times after that one, but you carried on, never gave up and it finally happened. How did that feel? What did you do differently each time, what attitude did you change to accomplish what you wanted? How did the experience change through all your efforts? Sometimes waiting for something you have longed for and worked hard for is worth all the more and you feel a greater sense of achievement.

⚘ Think of something at this very moment that you've always wanted to do. It could be something you want to learn, something you'd like to change in your life or within yourself, a person you'd like to meet, somewhere you'd like to go or a fear or challenge that you'd like to overcome. Many of us fear the thought of failure or we think we can't do it, so we never try. The saying goes, "If you never try, you'll never know". You'll never know how you'll feel or what something feels like until you try it. With every decision you make you change the course of your life. You may think your ideas and dreams are impossible, but give it a go, follow your instinct, dare to attempt the unthinkable, just go on and try, and if you slip then be grateful for a pleasant trip, see the lessons within it and try again. Perhaps your next attempt will take you down a completely different path altogether, one that you never thought was possible.

♡ It always helps to be surrounded by people who will support us in our dream to achieve or accomplish something. Gravitate towards people who have perhaps achieved something similar to your dream. Learn and read about the stories of people who have achieved something through much adversity to finally reach their goals. Be grateful for your own adversity towards your dreams. It is all part of the wonderful journey of discovery. Look for the lessons within each attempt at striving for something you want to achieve. Being grateful for the lesson will significantly affect your next attempt.

🧘 Think of something that you would love to achieve. In meditation, visualise, do a mental rehearsal of achieving what you want. It may not be actually happening, but you are changing the energy inside yourself and the energy outside yourself to attracting it into your life. As you visualise every scene, home your awareness into specific points, bring to life where you are, what's around you, the colours and textures around you, the people around you, what they are saying, what they are doing, how they are doing it. Notice the movement of your body. What are your thoughts, how are you feeling, involve all your senses, sight, sound, smell, taste and touch? Heighten every moment as if you are actually experiencing it. Your mind does not know the difference between what is thought and imagination, and what is reality. In that moment it is all completely real to you. To increase the quality of the whole experience, join your mind with your heart, generate feelings of gratitude. Feel your heart fill and expand with gratitude for what you are experiencing. Practice this exercise every day, each time increasing the details of the experience and increasing your feelings of gratitude. In your day-to-day life, start to watch out for signs that are guiding you to your destination, giving you the confidence to take measures to achieve what you want. It generally will turn out even better than you dreamed.

♡ Encourage someone you know that wants to do something but is afraid and does not believe in themselves. Remind them of examples of the things they have achieved and manifested in their life. Remind them of their many qualities. Motivate them along each step and encourage them to appreciate the progress they are making.

A Brand New Day

"For tomorrow belongs to the people who prepare for it today."
African Proverb

All our tomorrows are made up of today. We can be grateful for things which have not happened yet, we can be grateful for the brand new day ahead of us, for what we are going to experience and the way we are going to feel the following day.

We have many habit energies which pop up when we are faced with difficulties. We may respond to people and situations in a way that does not make us feel good and can create uncomfortable feelings within us and for those around us, and then our whole day is affected by this frame of mind. We can meditate on our tomorrow and make a conscious effort that whatever the day presents and however it unfolds we will be positive and deal with challenges with as much mindfulness, awareness, and kindness as possible. Today we can make a promise that tomorrow will be a day of mindfulness.

You may not succeed instantly, habit energies of responding a certain way to people and situations can be very hard to change just like that. If this happens don't feel bad about it or feel like you have failed, just be mindful of how you responded and be grateful that you noticed your response and try again next time. Always embrace any response either positive or negative with kindness. The fact that you are trying to be more mindful of your perceptions, attitude, reactions, and experiences is a great step in a wonderful new direction.

🧘 Meditate on tomorrow. It could be an average day at work, or you've planned a special day out or will be spending time with family and friends. Feel enthusiastic about tomorrow, imagine it going so well and being in a positive state of mind whatever happens. Imagine your perceptions change to other people's behaviours and responses and know that you will seek the wisdom inside yourself to approach any situation with ease and lightness and be grateful for whatever happens during the day.

♍ Choose a situation that you find yourself in regularly. It could be driving to and from work or something you do repetitively at work or at home. You may get tense by being in a particular situation, around a certain person or in a certain environment. Decide and make the intention today that tomorrow you will approach it with positivity and gratitude. In meditation visualise positive responses for tomorrow in this situation. Do the same for a person in your life that you want to change your response to. The power of intention, imagination, and visualisation can produce remarkable results. There is a saying from Max Planck, the originator of quantum physics. "When you change the way you look at things, the things you look at change". You may find through your positive power of intention and transforming your perceptions, the way the world appears to you, situations and people also change in a positive way around you. Enjoy experimenting with it, and see what unfolds through your positive intentions.

♡ Extend your experiences of happiness by anticipating well in advance, savouring it while it's happening, and then recalling your experience.

☺ Every morning when you wake up, give thanks for the twenty-four hours of a brand new day that has been gifted to you. Smile and look forward to the day ahead. Get excited about what you will experience during your day. Decide to do something differently to how you've done it before, generating a newness of experience.

♍ Choose one of the practices from this book the evening before you go to bed and look forward to practicing it the next day.

♍ Do a comparison of how you feel about something or someone today to how you felt about it or them the day before. Mentally note your progress. Notice how a brand new day makes a big difference in how you feel. Thank tomorrow for helping you feel better within yourself.

♍ Tomorrow doesn't have to be the next day; it can be the next moment. With every moment of our life, we can start again, learning from the previous moment to create a new positive, grateful moment. Remember to always be kind to yourself no matter what, every step of the way.

Continuation of our Ancestors

"If you look deeply into the palm of your hand, you will see your parents and all generations of your ancestors. All of them are alive in this moment. Each is present in your body. You are the continuation of each of these people." Thich Nhat Hanh

Most of us celebrate our birthday; the day we came out of our mother's womb and into the world and every year on the same date after that. We assume that this is our age and that we are a separate self, made up of the years and experiences of our individual lives. If we look deeply, we were also growing in our mother's womb for nine months before the day of coming out into the world. If we look even more deeply, we would not exist if it was not for our mother and father and they would not exist if it were not for their parents. We can go back through the many generations of our ancestors, through many hundreds and thousands of years to when humans evolved on our Planet. We could go further back still to all the creatures that evolved over the millions of years to then ultimately evolve into humans, not forgetting all the conditions around that helped bring about this evolution. So we can say that we are millions of years old. We are made up of all the many thousands of generations and conditions before us. We carry within us the essence of our ancestor's traits, their experiences, their learning, their journey, strength, and endurance through many lands to arrive at the land we live on today and to be the person we are today.

We cannot separate ourselves from our ancestors, they are in us and they continue in us and will continue within the many generations to come. Our feelings of respect and gratitude towards our ancestors can travel back thousands of generations to them because we inter-are, there is no separation. Our stream of gratitude flows back in time, touching each and every ancestor. We can send back our gratitude for all the gifts they have given us, for all their hard work to raise their families, for all the experience and wisdom they have passed on through the many generations to reach us.

◊ A beautiful tradition within Vietnamese culture is paying of respect to ancestors by keeping an ancestral altar in the home. You can create your own ancestral altar in your home, a place where you can honour your ancestors. Place photos, flowers, candles, items belonging to your ancestors, something symbolic or something you've made symbolising your respect and gratitude to your ancestors.

✎ Write a love letter to your parents, grandparents or other relatives. Your letter could include -

- The positive special qualities that they possess, all the things you love, admire and respect about them.
- Special things they've taught you that have helped you in your life.
- What you've learnt from them and how it's helped you watching them overcome a challenging experience and how you admire them for it.
- Thank them for all the qualities and skills that you've inherited from them and let them know how you are getting on now.

Feel grateful for all the wonderful gifts your ancestors hold and what they have passed on to you. After you've written your letter you can light a candle for them. If the family member you have chosen is still present, you can give them your letter or even read it out to them.

♡ Go back even further to your ancestral roots. Did your ancestors live in another country? What would their lives have been like then and what kind of work did they do? Do some research; ask your family about them, what traits do you feel you have inherited from your distant ancestors? Feel grateful for all the special qualities and gifts that have been passed down the many generations to you, keeping an awareness that your ancestors are still very much alive in you today.

❋ Plant an ancestral tree or a flowering plant as a symbol of your gratitude to the lives of your ancestors. Remember your ancestors each time you tend and nurture the plant or tree as it grows.

Dear Friends

"A friend is one that knows you as you are, understands where you have been, accepts what you have become, and still, gently allows you to grow." William Shakespeare

What would we do without our friends? Good friends are there for us when we need support, they listen and understand, they cheer us up when we need a lift in spirit; we laugh and enjoy wonderful moments together and even share moments of silence. True friendship is a beautiful gift, like having a kindred spirit, the family that we have chosen. Sometimes we can be more of our true selves with friends than we are with our own family. We feel we can talk more openly and honestly and show our true spirit when we are around our friends.

Friends first come together because of a shared interest or experience and eventually they embrace and celebrate their differences. Supporting us, encouraging us, inspiring us and cheering us on to fulfil our dreams. Our friends help us when we are facing difficult life challenges. True friendship takes us by the hand and reminds us that we are not alone on the journey.

Throughout our lives, we have many friends. Some we have known for most of our lives since childhood, other friendships are fleeting but have made a great impact on our lives. If a friendship ended for whatever reason, nothing was really lost; instead, we must be grateful for the experience of knowing a person with whom we had a great connection; someone who has enhanced our life in some way. There are countless wonderful and creative ways to show our appreciation to our friends.

♡ When a friend is in need, be there for them, by making time to listen attentively to their worries, only occasionally speaking to offer an alternative positive interpretation.

♡ Encourage a friend to try something you know they want to try but haven't yet because they're afraid.

♡ Arrange a day with your friend or a few friends and make it a friendship day. International Friendship Day is on 30th July, but you can make your own friendship day any time. Choose something you all would like to do together for the day and celebrate your friendships. You could also invite a friend to do something you know they've always wanted to do and you would like to help them fulfil their dream.

✎ Send or give a "Thank you" card to a friend and write in it how much you are grateful to them. Write something specific about them, a wonderful trait, a thoughtful act, something they said or did that you are grateful for. Compliment them on a talent, skill, or strength that you admire. Share a specific example of something they did for you or said to you and how it made a positive difference in your life. Hand making your own card shows that you've made a special effort for the appreciation of that person. A nice idea is to make a card with a photo of you and your friend on it with your message inside.

♡ Give them something of yours that you think they would enjoy and let them know specifically why you want them to have it.

♡ Share something positive about a friend while talking about them to other people.

♡ Do something thoughtful for them, such as make them a nice meal or help them with a chore. As a gesture of your appreciation, ask them if they need any help with something, in particular, making it clear that it would be a way of showing your gratitude for their friendship.

♡ Many of us give gifts to friends during birthdays or special occasions. Give a gift to a friend on a random day just because you are grateful to them, again making a gift is even more special. It doesn't have to cost much, it's always the gifts that have creativity and thoughtfulness put into them that are remembered and treasured the most.

♟ Make a list of all the friends you have; friends from the past and present. In meditation or written down think of something you appreciate about them. Send them your feelings of gratitude.

My Spirit Within

"Everything has a spirit - honour that." Native American saying

Humans possess natural innate beautiful qualities which blossom at various times during their lives. There are so many qualities within us that we can be grateful for. Qualities and virtues that have helped us with our achievements, moments that we can be proud of, kindness and generosity towards others, learning a new skill, courage, patience, strength and much more. Our spirit manifests itself in many ways; through our thoughts, our words, and our actions, towards ourselves, others and our environment.

If we meditate on all our qualities and virtues we would have a very long list. There are so many things that are not obvious to us but when we look deeply at the things we have done, the people we have helped including ourselves, how we have helped the environment, our achievements and all the hobbies and pastimes and activities we like to do and the qualities required to do all of these things we would find many reasons to be grateful to ourselves, for our spirit within.

✎ Make a list of things that you love to do, that you have a passion for. It could be hobbies or activities, work-related or family-and-friends related; anything that brings you happiness, joy, contentment or a sense of achievement and purpose. Now choose one from your list and write it in the centre of a large piece of paper. Draw a symbol of your choice around it; a circle, a flower, a heart, a tree, a Sun, anything you like. From the symbol in the centre of the paper draw lines coming out, you can make this as colourful as you like. On these lines write down all the qualities, virtues and skills that you have within you that are needed to love what you do. Refer to the list of qualities on the following page to help you.

For example, if you love travelling, you are adventurous, have courage, an interest in meeting different people and learning about different cultures. If you love gardening, you are nurturing, caring, hardworking, and patient, you have an appreciation for nature and its beauty and you have peace. If you love sport, you care about your health, you are energetic. If you love teaching, you want to pass on knowledge and skills to others, you have patience and you are caring and want to help others. If you love art, you have an appreciation for colour, texture, shape, and form and you are patient and have an eye for detail. Fill the page or pages up with all the things you love to do and attach your qualities to them. Feel grateful for the abundance of qualities you possess.

✏ Do the same exercise as above for all your achievements. For example, if you passed a test, write down all the qualities in you that helped you pass the test, think of all the qualities you needed to have studied or practiced to achieve something.

✏ Make another list of things you have done to help people. Write down all the qualities that you have within you to be able to help people. For example, you may have been there for a friend, volunteered, helped a stranger. It requires wanting to share your happiness, joy, generosity, care, and love. When we have been hurt by someone, we show great understanding and insight, we are able to care for ourselves by being able to forgive and find peace. You will see the page fill up with a multitude of qualities that you possess. Feel grateful for the beauty within yourself.

⚜ Become aware of the qualities you are demonstrating while you are doing something or feeling something in the present moment.

⚜ What's the next small step you want to take? What dreams, aspirations, and goals do you have? If you have an aim to achieve something, look at all the qualities you need, the first step, the small steps towards it. Which qualities do you need to encourage within yourself? Seize any opportunities that come your way to help develop the qualities needed, start to notice the qualities that you already have and water and develop them within yourself to achieve your goal, grateful for every part of the journey and for every quality in yourself.

♡ Say "I love you", "I am grateful" to yourself from time to time or when you really need it. Appreciate who you really are. If we can truly love and appreciate ourselves we can truly love others and the world around us.

Seeds of Gratitude

♡ We all possess every wonderful quality there is. All of them are like seeds within us. Some of these qualities/seeds are listed on the opposite page. Choose 3 qualities from the list that you feel best describe you.

♡ Starting from the beginning of the list, meditate on the meaning of the quality. Look up the definition in a dictionary to give you a better idea if you like. Choose one quality a day and think of a situation in your life in which you expressed this quality.

♡ Practice with a friend, partner or family member. Choose one of the qualities from the list and share with each other an example of how you've demonstrated or expressed this quality in your life.

♡ Each day choose a quality that you wish to demonstrate, express or encourage during your day. At the end of the day re-evaluate what you did and feel grateful for the quality and how it made you feel.

♡ Practising with a friend, partner or family member, pick 3 qualities that you feel describes them the best and explain why you've chosen these specific qualities.

♡ Think of a person that you are having some challenges or disagreements with. Choose 3 qualities from the list that you feel they possess and think of ways they demonstrate them. Through your heart send them your gratitude for these qualities.

♡ Choose a quality to concentrate and meditate on during physical activities like walking, yoga, tai-chi, breathing exercises, sports, cooking, cleaning, and gardening. Bring this quality into your activity. Embody, nurture, encourage, become this quality while you practice what you are doing. Use your body and the activity to water the seeds of this quality within you. Allow the quality/seed to sit in your heart and grow slowly, spreading its energy out in all directions.

Acceptance	Determination	Honesty	Openness	Silence
Adventure	Discipline	Hopeful	Optimism	Simplicity
Appreciation	Easiness	Hospitality	Originality	Sincerity
Aspiration	Empowerment	Humility	Passion	Smile
Authenticity	Endurance	Humour	Patience	Spirit
Balance	Enthusiasm	Insight	Peace	Spontaneity
Beauty	Faith	Integrity	Perception	Stability
Boldness	Faithfulness	Intelligence	Perseverance	Strength
Calm	Fearlessness	Introspection	Positivity	Surrender
Caring	Flexibility	Intuition	Prayer	Thoughtfulness
Cheerfulness	Forgiveness	Joyfulness	Presence	Tolerance
Comfortable	Freedom	Kindness	Punctuality	Transformation
Commitment	Friendship	Knowledge	Purpose	Trust
Communication	Generosity	Laughter	Reason	Truth
Compassion	Gentleness	Lightness	Resilience	Understanding
Concentration	Good Wishes	Listening	Respect	Vulnerability
Confidence	Goodness	Love	Responsibility	Wellbeing
Contentment	Gratefulness	Loyalty	Rest	Will
Cooperation	Happiness	Maturity	Sacredness	Wisdom
Courage	Harmony	Mindfulness	Self-Respect	Wonder
Creativity	Healing	Nurture	Serenity	Young at Heart

Doing My Bit

"I alone cannot change the world. But I can cast a stone across the waters to create many ripples." Mother Teresa

We all have the capacity to make a difference. No matter how big or small it may appear to be. We cannot fix all the troubles in the world, but we can contribute in our own way to help make the world a better place. Feel grateful for the part you are playing, for the bit you are doing to help. Appreciate that what you are doing matters. If everyone did their bit, it would generate a collective conscious effort which creates a greater impact on the world.

🧘 Acknowledge and value one thing that you do to help others; your family, the environment, your community, the world. Feel grateful to yourself for doing it. Look more deeply at how what you do has a ripple effect on the people and the world around you. Look at how you are contributing in so many more ways than you had ever realised.

🧘 Celebrate what others are doing to help the world. Observe and become aware of other people's contribution, at doing their bit. Notice and perhaps even express your gratitude to them. Make them aware of the positive impact they are having on the world through their thoughts and actions.

🧘 Our grateful and positive thoughts also have a great impact on the people and the world around us. Our thoughts carry a vibration which affects the environment around us. We can be doing our bit when we practice gratitude, by cultivating and sending positive thoughts to ourselves and the world around us.

🧘 Think of something that you'd like to do to help. Make that extra effort in helping another or the environment, your community, through thoughts, words or actions. Don't forget that doing something to help yourself is a noble thing. Know within your heart that you are doing a great thing; that your energy of love and kindness sends ripples across an endless ocean, which transforms into an unlimited source of gratitude.

The Fragrance of Gratitude

"Don't hurry, don't worry. You're only here for a short visit. So don't forget to stop and smell the roses." Walter Hagen

The sense of smell is powerful in evoking memories. Because we encounter most new odours in our youth, smells often call up childhood memories. A smell can bring on a flood of memories, influence a person's mood and even affect work performance. A smell can call up memories and powerful responses almost instantaneously. A smell is an invisible energy essence which softly sends messages to us about its surroundings.

Smells connected with food are particularly evoking. Have you ever noticed how food tastes different when you have a cold? Smell and taste are inextricably connected. What we perceive as "taste" actually results from our sense of smell. Our sense of smell also triggers the release of enzymes and other substances that will eventually break down food to release the nutrient inside. The body then burns these nutrients for energy or uses them to build new tissues and body parts. How many times has the smell of certain foods set your tummy rumbling? These are the enzymes starting to work before any food has even reached the stomach.

🍎 Before you dive straight into your meal, take a little time to savour the smell of the food. Allow the scent to start the digestive juices flowing to help maximise nutrient absorption into your cells.

🧘 Do the smell meditation – Use the power of the mind to evoke the smell of something without the direct experience of it. Choose something you already have experienced the smell of. Close your eyes and visualise this particular object, person, and place; anything that evokes strong memories for you. Remembering the smell, how does the smell make you feel? What emotions are you experiencing? What memories is it conjuring up?

❀ Choose a fragrant flower to do a meditation on, drink in its essence.

Music, the Voice of the Soul

"The music is not in the notes, but in the silence between." Wolfgang Amadeus Mozart

For many people and within many cultures, music is an important part of life. Music is a common chord that weaves through every culture, a soul language. Vocal or instrumental sounds, or both, are combined in such a way as to produce beauty of form, harmony, and expression of emotion. Many of us simply enjoy listening to the sounds, melodies, and rhythms that music brings to our ears, minds, and hearts. We listen to music to relax, and we love to dance to music, to express our joy and move our bodies to the rhythm of the sounds. Music and song are a pure dialogue of emotion and can stir up feelings in us and it can lift us up to a happier joyous place. Listening to certain music and songs can remind us of an important time in our lives, they touch us emotionally, where words alone cannot. Music can transform us on the deepest level.

♫ When you have a quiet moment in your day choose one of your favourite songs or instrumentals and really listen carefully to it. Engage yourself fully. Listen to the sounds of the instruments, the melody, the rhythm, the expression of emotion; how many instruments can you hear? The singing voice is also an instrument. Choose one of those instruments and listen carefully to the sound of it. Listen to how all the instruments work so well together to produce the wonderful blend of music and sounds. Close your eyes, now you are listening to the music fully without any other external input. Become aware of how all the sounds are heightened when you close your eyes. The music is now inside your mind and body and you are one with the sounds. How does the music make you feel? What emotions does it conjure up?

♫ Move your body to the music. You could dance where people usually dance to music, such as a party or a concert, in a dance class or it could be in the privacy of your own home; dance alone or with others. Allow your body to become another instrument of the music and express your love and joy for the sounds and music through your body.

♫ Whenever you listen to music that you like, feel grateful for all the artists that created the music and wrote the song. Think of all the people who would have been involved in creating the music; all the musicians, the singers, the artists, the songwriters, the producers, technicians and all the instruments themselves. Feel a great appreciation for those who invented and made the instruments which created the sounds. They all have played their part in sharing their talent, expression of emotion and sound with us; they have awakened our spirit and given us great enjoyment and depth of feeling.

♫ Sing along to songs you like when you can; in your home, in the car, in the shower, in the kitchen, in a show or concert, on your own or with your family and friends. It doesn't matter if you are not the greatest of singers, just singing along can make you feel connected to the music and words and helps you to express the joy and emotion within yourself. Start singing and encourage those around you to sing along too. It will increase the joy and gratitude of everyone who joins in.

♫ Share your love for music with people you care about. Choose a song or instrumental that expresses how you feel about a person you love. Listen to the song together or send them the song or tell them the name of the song so they can listen to it from where they are. If you play an instrument or sing, you could write your own music and sing your own song to the person you love or record it for them. Music and song are beautiful ways to express your love and gratitude to someone.

♫ When you are listening to a song, let the sentiments of the song stir up any feelings of something you are or need to be grateful for. What feelings arise from them, what message are they conveying?

♫ Share the experience of listening to music with your family or friends or in a show with many people. Connect with those around you where everyone's feelings and emotions are synchronised with the music.

♫ If you need a lift of spirit, listen to your favourite inspirational songs. Try and apply into your life the message that the songs are conveying. Choose a theme song for each week to focus your practice on.

The Colours of the Sun

The world around us is filled with a tapestry of colours. We sense colour through our eyes and our brain and from objects by the way it absorbs, reflects or emits light. Each colour has a different wave-like frequency of light. All the colours that we see around us are dependent on a rainbow spectrum of light from the Sun, an object to look at and our visual system – our eyes and brain.

The human eye can distinguish approximately 10 million different colours. Studies have shown that not everyone sees all the same colours, it all depends on the kinds of colour receptors we have in our eyes and on how much we pay attention to colours. Artists can perceive a wider range of colours. Studies show that our eyes will develop the sensors to be able to detect more colours around us if we are more mindful of their many subtle shades. There are many indigenous cultures that are able to see different colours depending on their environment.

Colour can affect our mood. Vibrant colours can lift our mood and make us feel happier. Some colours can make us feel more relaxed. Feel gratitude for the abundance of colours all around, grateful for the Sun's light, and for your eyes and brain which allow you to perceive these colours. When you are mindful and grateful of particular colours, what you look at takes on a completely different dimension.

🧘 Close your eyes for a few minutes, then open them and see how the colours around you are so much richer, vibrant, sharper and brighter. Feel grateful for your eyes and the light; to be able to see the wonderful world around you. What a beautiful gift it is!

🦋 Capture colour in a photo. With a digital camera or your mobile phone, take photos of colourful objects, places, things, people, landscapes you are grateful for. Take photos of something in nature; flowers are so wonderfully rich in colour; try colourful objects in markets or food, clothes, art.

❋ Nature reflects the most beautiful colours. Place your attention on different aspects of nature and their colours. The multitude of colours in flowers, the many shades of green in the many forms of trees and plants; in the leaves, in the grasses, amongst the hills. See how the colours change during different seasons and during different times of the day and to different levels of light from the Sun. When the Sun is high in the sky the colours are different from when the Sun is low in the sky. Become more mindful of how different conditions of light produce different colours in the same object that you are looking at.

⚜ Choose a colour to concentrate on and look out for in your daily life.

🦋 Create your own art using colour – paint, draw, knit, create a mosaic or a collage of images, and make things using different coloured paper. Mix colours in paint and see what new colours are formed.

🦋 Colourful clothes and accessories are a very important part of many cultures. Choose items of clothing and certain accessories that are more colourful. Wear one item of clothing that stands out from the rest or choose one piece of accessory that you love the colour of.

🦋 Place your eyes on a particular object or part of an object and really look at the colours within it, absorb the colour into your mind and body with your eyes. How does it make you feel? Does it remind you of anything? Which colours do you really like? Which colours lift your mood? Which colours relax you?

🍎 Food contains a wonderful array of colours. Naturally brightly colourful foods are healthier for us, containing protective antioxidants. When preparing meals, try and include a wide variety of colour in your meals. These colours are absorbed by your body and their healthy properties become part of you.

🦋 It's important to embrace all colours. There may be a colour you don't particularly like for some reason; ignite your curiosity for the colour by looking out for it in the world around you and find creative ways to incorporate it into your life. Learn to love the colour you at first turned away from.

The Sound of Silence

"See how nature – trees, flowers, grass, grow in silence; see the stars, the Moon, and the Sun, how they move in silence... We need silence to be able to touch souls." Mother Teresa

Silence is a space which allows us to become still within ourselves and hear the sound of the wisdom, the inner voice that resides deep within us. Silence heightens our ability to truly understand ourselves, to really listen to what our mind and heart are saying and to allow our higher inner self to guide our thoughts, feelings, words, and actions onto a path that is true and wise. Silence allows our spirit to be nurtured, to learn, grow strong and bloom. Being in a space of quietness increases our creativity, allows us to listen to our intuition; it is where we can be inspired, and where insight is born.

Silence is very important in meditation practice. To sit and be still with eyes closed allows all our senses to be at rest, allowing our minds to slow down and concentrate on our inner selves.

Silence is also important in prayer, allowing our mind to send positive and healing thoughts to people we love, to people we want to make peace with, to people in other nations and to ourselves.

Nature is a beautiful place to appreciate silence, allowing the stillness of the natural surroundings to bring us peace. The silence of nature is reflected back into our mind, body, heart, and spirit, bringing us back to our true selves.

Every day we are surrounded by many different kinds of noises from many different sources, but there are also many places and situations in which we may find ourselves in silence. When these moments occur, take the opportunity to enjoy and feel grateful for the silence; grateful for the peace and calm. Feel comfortable in the silence, savour it and make it your friend. Allow the silence to slowly permeate your whole being and listen carefully to what it is teaching you.

⚭ Choose a time in your day to find silence. When the opportunity arises, sit or stand in a place where it is silent or find the quietest place you can. This could be while at work, or at home, in nature, or it could be while you are in the bathroom if this is the only place you can find a quiet place. Almost anywhere where there is very little noise and you are on your own. The silence creates space and allows the thoughts in your mind to slow down and you become more aware of your body being still. Concentrating on your breathing also helps you feel calmer and more present. You find yourself slowly merging with the silence. In a day which can be so filled with noise, enjoy the silence and come back to the stillness inside yourself, feel gratitude for the peace. If you find that your mind starts to wonder gently bring your awareness back to your breathing. In this place of silence, feel the space around you expanding.

❋ Find a place to sit and be with nature. Keeping your eyes open, feel the silence of your surroundings. See how nature lives so beautifully in peace. Look up at the sky and see the stillness of the blue sky or how the clouds move silently in slow motion. Look at a tree or a flower; observe the stillness of the natural surroundings. Silence is the wisdom of nature. Just as a great teacher who sits before us in silence, we can learn more from silence than from any spoken words. We have the inner wisdom that will guide us when we are able to listen to the sound and wisdom of silence. Feel grateful for what nature is teaching you and for the wisdom that is born from its quietness.

♡ When we are in the company of others, we often feel the need to speak, to make conversation; we can become uncomfortable with the silence. But being silent with someone or a group of people can be a very deep experience. Meditate, be mindful, pray or be in nature with someone or a group of people and enjoy the silence together. This shared collective energy of silent mindfulness deepens the whole experience and allows us to feel more connected with those around us.

⚭ Sit in a fairly quiet place, close your eyes and focus on listening to the sounds around you. Gradually shift your focus to the silence between the sounds. Allow a deeper stillness to permeate your consciousness.

A Sense of the World

Our senses can help to remind us of something to be grateful for. They can trigger a thought or a memory from deep within our subconscious mind and bring it into the present moment. When we see a photo of someone we know, it brings the thoughts and feelings of that person into our minds and hearts. When we see a photo of a place where we have been, it brings back some of our memories of our experience during that time and our feelings about the time and place are felt once more. A smell can take us back to a time in our past and to how we felt or remind us of a person, place or experience. Taste can do the same. Perhaps you ate or drank something which takes you back to a time and place when you last had that food or drink and were grateful for it. Music is a wonderful reminder of the past. We are surrounded by music as we grow up. When we hear a song from our past we are immediately transported back to a time in our past. We can relate to the words of songs, we relate them to a time in our life; they can bring back our feelings again from our past, either happy or sad. Touch is also very important as a reminder of gratitude. When we hold and feel something with our hands and fingers, thoughts can come up from our lives relating to what we are touching. Almost everything in our lives has been experienced through our senses at some point and stored in our memories. All of these reminders are like bells of mindfulness. A bell is something which makes us stop and notice; it is a reminder to bring our minds back to the present moment and in that present moment we can look more deeply into things and feel grateful for them.

◊ Place reminders of gratitude around your home or work or anywhere you spend a lot of time, where you will see them most often. These reminders can be words, photos, objects or symbols. Photos of people you know and places you've been words, quotes, a welcome sign or thank you sign, cards, posters, paintings, all having something significant in them to help remind you to be grateful of something. Choose a particular object as your trigger to become aware of your surroundings.

🍎 Become aware of what you can smell while you are cooking. Select an ingredient one at a time and smell it, grateful for its contribution to your meal. Herbs and spices have the most wonderful odour. When eating food, take your time to appreciate the smells it releases. Does the smell of a particular food remind you of anything? Absorb the wonderful colours and textures that make up the meal you are preparing.

🍎 When you eat or drink something, what does it taste like; does it remind you of a memorable happy time in your life for which you are grateful? Close your eyes while eating or drinking something. What thoughts and feelings emerge from within you?

🧘 Bring your awareness to your sense of touch. While walking we touch our feet on the ground, we feel the Earth beneath us. This is a reminder to be grateful for our feet as well as to being able to walk and have gratitude for the Earth we are walking on. Touching something with our hands and fingers is a reminder of gratitude for what we are holding. Feel its shape and texture, look at its colours, smell it. Looking deeply at the object in our hand we can find even more things to be grateful for.

🧘 Challenge your senses – rather than eat a certain food with a spoon, knife or fork, eat it with your hands. Rather than look at an object in your hands, close your eyes and feel it, smell it, use your other senses. When you see something that is wonderful, what tastes does it conjure up in you? When you hear something, words or music or sounds from the natural world, what do you see in your mind? When you smell certain foods, what tastes in your mouth are produced? Have fun with your senses. Change the sense you would usually use and replace it with another and see what happens.

🧘 Intuition is known are the sixth sense. Become more aware of what your intuition is saying. Learn to more attune to it and trust in it.

🧘 Each day spend a few minutes to really take in the sounds around you. Dive into the natural sensation of hearing. Try closing your eyes to really bring your hearing to the forefront.

Stick-it Happy

A sticky note will stick almost anywhere. Nowadays they come in all colours, sizes, shapes, and themes. They are simple but perfect little things to use to help us cultivate gratitude.

✏ Use sticky notes as reminders. Write down something you want to be grateful for on a sticky note and stick it somewhere in your home, car or at work. Somewhere you know you will see it at least once a day. When you see the note it will prompt you to feel more grateful, be more mindful of whatever you have written on it. You can choose a different subject each day, week or month or stick several sticky notes around your home or workplace as reminders.

♡ Use sticky notes to write little messages of gratitude to someone. Leave them in places where they can see them, like in a book they are reading, on their computer, in the kitchen cupboard, on a favourite mug, on a mirror, on a table, on a door. It will put a smile on your face and brighten someone's day.

🦋 Encourage children to use sticky notes at home and within a classroom. Use a wall in your home to stick notes. Children can write down something they are grateful for or positive words and make a collage of sticky gratitude notes; and of course, this is also a great practice for adults too. Use colourful pens and different coloured, shaped sticky notes to make it more attractive.

✏ Stick "Thank you" sticky notes on items around your home that you are grateful for. You can write about how you are grateful for the item or simply "Thank you".

✏ Put sticky note in places where you'll find them at some time in the future to remind you of something you were grateful for in the past.

♡ Place gratitude sticky notes in random places where people can read them prompting an activation of gratitude within others.

Scraps of Gratitude

"It is not joy that makes us grateful; it is gratitude that makes us joyful."
Brother David Steindl-Rast

❈ Create a scrapbook of things you are grateful for. Buy a book of any size and stick photos, cards, printed images, artwork, gifts, letters, quotes, drawings, magazine cut-outs; all to remind you of what you are grateful for. Be as creative and inventive as you like.

❈ Create a gratitude box. Gratitude boxes are another great way to keep items which remind us of something to be grateful for. Small items such as little gifts given by others or a memento of a lovely day out, a ticket, cards, and letters, something you have picked up from nature, anything small which generates gratefulness in your heart.

❈ You can dedicate a part of a wall in your home to put up a scrap board and place photos, images, art, cards, quotes of things you are grateful for. Every time you place your eyes on the board you will be reminded of something to be grateful for. Others who see the board may then also be encouraged to create their own gratitude scrap board in their home.

❈ Create a scrapbook, gratitude box, mobile scrapbook or photo book for a friend or family member, containing memorable photos of times spent together. Make up a collection of memorable items or symbols from times spent together. Give it to them as your grateful gift.

❈ Create a gratitude scrapbook, scrap box, mobile scrapbook, wall scrap board, including images or items of things, places or experiences you would love to manifest in the future. Create your future by bringing the energy of gratitude for the future into the present moment. Get excited for what you would like to manifest as if it actually will happen or that it has already happened. By doing this you are getting excited about the future, generating and drawing the future towards you.

And the Award Goes To....

The purpose of an award is to celebrate achievements; to recognise, acknowledge, honour and show appreciation to individuals for their great effort, skill and significant contributions in a particular area. Giving awards help to encourage and motivate individuals on their path.

We can make our gratitude practice creative and fun by awarding the people, animals, achievements, and things we appreciate in our life.

♡ Take something that you use a lot of, for instance, your car. Think of all the things that your car does for you, all the effort it's made to take you from place to place, how it keeps you safe and protected. You can meditate on the wonderful things about your car, write them down or talk to someone about them. Give your car an excellent service award for outstanding achievement. Pamper your car with a mindful grateful wash, clean the inside, and take it for a service.

♡ You can have faithful companionship awards for pets and people in your life. With pets, you can award them with a pampering day. Spend quality time with a friend, give them something that will make them happy, cook them a lovely meal, give them a plant or flowers, write them a card or letter, make them something special. Think of something that will make them feel special and appreciated. Think of it as your grateful award to them.

☺ Choose a part of your body to award for outstanding health service achievement; for example your lungs. Think of all the amazing things about your lungs, how strong they must be, how they allow you to breathe in clean air, pumping oxygen into your body and cells and releasing waste and toxins. How can we reward our lungs? They would love to breathe in fresh clean air, so go for a walk somewhere fresh. You could also do deep abdominal breathing to really help expand your lungs to take in increased oxygen and release trapped waste. You could also sing a song or have a good laugh to exercise your lungs.

☺ Other ways to award your body are by giving yourself a good massage or by getting a massage. Research the foods and drinks which help your body – you can treat your internal organs such as your intestines with a meal which helps cleanse the colon, you can treat your liver with a liver cleansing drink, your cells with more water, your skin with moisturising oils, your teeth with a new toothbrush or mouthwash or give them a good thorough clean and floss or go to the dentists to have them cleaned thoroughly. You can award your muscles and whole body with a walk or stretching exercises. There are countless imaginative ways you can award and treat your body and show it your gratitude for its ongoing service to you.

◊ You could have excellent household service award ceremonies for outstanding services to items such as cooking pots, the washing machine, telephone, cooker, etc. You could give them a good clean to show your appreciation or talk to others about how these items help you in your life.

◊ Hold award ceremonies for your home or garden. Give your home a spring clean, put on your green fingers and give your garden some love and attention, award it with a new plant or ornament, give it a good water, go round your home and garden and thank parts of it to show your appreciation. You could make something for the house or garden and hold a dedication ceremony, make a speech and present your award. Create a table centrepiece of house plants, leaves, acorns, rocks, to show your gratitude for the gifts of nature.

◊ You also deserve awards. Hold your own award ceremony for a special quality that you possess or a quality that came through for you when most needed; for helping people in need, for achieving something that took a great deal of courage and effort, for dealing with a difficult situation well. Treat yourself to something special or write a speech to yourself and hold a ceremony.

◊ Life most definitely deserves an award; the life that you've been given and the life that is all around you. In a group share what you love most about life and being alive. Make something special to award life and conduct your own ceremony.

Gratitude Jar

Writing down our gratitude each day is a wonderful way of preserving our feelings, thoughts, and experiences. A way to make this more fun and memorable is to write something you are grateful for on pieces of paper and put them in a jar. This is something you can do for yourself, with your partner or with your family; children will love this practice.

✎ Decorate a jar and label it. It would need to be large enough to place your hand inside; you could call it the 'Gratitude Jar' or any other creative name. Place small pieces of paper next to the jar or nearby to write your messages of gratitude on and a nice pen. To make it more fun you can cut the pieces of paper in different shapes and use different coloured paper and place them in a bowl next to the jar. Each day, write down something you are grateful for. After you have written your gratitude, fold up the piece of paper and place it into the jar. At the end of a period of time or when the jar is full you can dip your fingers into the jar, take out one of the pieces of paper and read and remind yourself of your gratitude. It's a wonderful way to preserve your feelings and also to share with others your gratitude if you choose. If as a family you have created the gratitude jar, you can all take turns to dip into the jar and say out loud what's written for everyone to hear and appreciate as well.

✎ Make a personal gratitude jar for someone you love. Write down what you are grateful for in a particular person, it could be about things they have done that you are grateful for, or just for being the person they are or anything they would love to read. It could also be for someone who needs a lift in spirit. When it's full, give them the jar as a gift, it will make them feel so appreciated and happy. It's a wonderful way to share your gratitude with someone you love and care about, and also helps encourage them to be more grateful in their own life.

✎ On 52 different pieces of paper write 52 different gratitude practices and place them in a jar. Each week pick one out and practice what's written on it as much as possible all week long.

Alphabet Games

Start from A and go all the way through to Z. Think of something you are grateful for beginning with the letter you are on. You can do this on your own, with someone else, with children, in meditation or you can write them down or say them out loud. It could be anything that pops into your head, such as a thing, a place, a person, a event, an experience, a feeling, an animal, a colour, a food, a state of mind, a dream that you hold, something from the past or something from the present moment, even something from the future, anything that brings up feelings of gratitude that begins with that letter. The letters Q, X and Z may be a challenge, so I suggest thinking of something that contains the letter Q, X or Z rather than starts with this letter. You can always use the internet or the dictionary to help you find a word.

While going through the alphabet you can concentrate on a particular subject, such as positive qualities or virtues that people have, like A for Appreciation, B for Balance, C for Co-operation, etc. Other subject areas are nature, food, the body, friends, and family. Choose a subject now – start with A for.....

Use the letters of the alphabet to practice 26 days of gratitude. Use one letter for each day and make that the focus of your gratitude for that day. Choose a gratitude practice or a meditation of something or someone beginning with that particular letter; create your own or choose one from this book. An example for day one: A for Air – practice being grateful for the air all around us, the air we breathe in, do a breathing meditation; throughout your day become mindful of the air around you.

Create your own gratitude dictionary, adding new words as they arise, expanding a little more as to why you are grateful for each word and what it represents.

Make an alphabet playing card set. Create a card for each letter of the alphabet. Each person picks a card and says something they are grateful for beginning with the letter they have chosen and explains why they are grateful for it.

A Picture Paints a Thousand Words

One picture can convey more to someone than a thousand words. Pictures can be in the form of photos, film, paintings or sketches or any form of visual art. When we take a photo we capture that moment and feeling in time and it is preserved in the photo. We store the moment in a photo so we can look at it at any time and feel again the same essence of the emotion of that moment. We capture our fascination, our joy, our love; we capture the world around us, its beauty and form. We capture the smiles of our loved ones; we capture the beauty of the moment. A painting or a sketch takes a great deal of observation, mindfulness, time and effort to create. Each stroke captures the subtle colours, shapes, and forms, the very essence of what has been observed and created. When we look at any piece of visual art, we see what the artist who created the picture sees through their eyes but also we conjure up our own feelings about what we are looking at. It tells us a story without words.

🦋 Pictures of all forms are around us everywhere. Look around you now and you'll see a picture somewhere. Start observing pictures around you more deeply, give them more of your attention. If you find one that you are particularly attracted to, one that draws you in, keep your attention on it for a while. Look at the colours, textures, light, and forms within it. What do you most like about it? Become mindful of how it makes you feel. What feelings are arising in you? What elements within the picture symbolise something that you can be or are grateful for? Do the same exercise by going to places where they exhibit paintings, photography or other forms of visual art. Stand before a piece of art for a while and give it your full attention.

🦋 If you love painting or sketching or even if you've never tried it before, paint or sketch something you are grateful for; something you love and find fascinating.

🦋 Create a photo gratitude book. Take a photo every day or once a week of something that you are grateful for, print it out and stick it in a book, you could write a line description of the photo or more if you like or leave it blank as the picture will carry the essence of what you are grateful for.

Create a photo book online with digital photos. You could share your photos with friends and family on a free blog. You could also take photos on your mobile phone and save them on your phone in a gratitude folder. Give yourself a challenge of taking a gratitude photo every day or even once a week, you'll begin to really start seeing things to be grateful for that you never noticed before. You will become more aware and mindful and find creative ways to convey what you are grateful for in a photo.

As well as your own photos you could cut out pictures you find in magazines which capture something you are grateful for, or you can take pictures off the internet to create your gratitude book, pictures you connect with and that convey your appreciation for something.

Become a filmmaker; create your own gratitude film. Start by taking short films either from your mobile or any other filming device of things, people, experiences you are grateful for. You can also choose a subject area and take films relating to it. At the end put the pieces of films together using a film editor. You can find free movie maker apps for your mobile. If you wish, select some background music. Share your creative gratitude film with friends and family. Perhaps it will encourage them to do one of their own and share it with others.

Create a future picture project. What would you like to manifest in your future – a place to visit, an experience, a job, better health, a person you'd like to meet. Create your own visual art, painting, photos, sketches, gratitude picture book, a film, a collage of pictures representing or symbolising what you really wish for. While creating your project generate the emotions and feelings of appreciation for your future and the great abundance that is yet to come as if it has already arrived.

Gather a group and ask everyone to bring in an image of something they are grateful for, each person shares and expresses their gratitude for it to the rest of the group.

Motion Pictures

Bring your gratitude practice into your viewing of motion pictures. Motion pictures in the form of films on television, documentaries, comedy, and films on the big screen at the cinema.

⚜ As the narrative progresses immerse yourself into the story. Pay attention to the images on the screen, the expressions on people's faces, their emotions. What emotions do you feel while watching? Notice the sensations in your body. Does your body language change as you watch? Do you tense up at exciting moments? How do you feel while watching touching moments? Being mindful while watching can result in a more fulfilling viewing experience.

⚜ While watching a motion picture, ask yourself 'What am I learning from this. What life lessons can I take away from this film? Think about how you can apply what you've learned into your life.

⚜ Watch one of your favourite inspirational films again. What you do love most about it and why? Has the film influenced the choices you've made in your life or helped shape your life in some way? While watching the film again is there anything new you've noticed which you can apply to your own life.

🦋 Create your own motion picture story in your mind and perhaps even write a screenplay. Let your imagination guide your story. What characters will be in your story, what are the messages you would like to convey in your narrative and imagery? Picture the details of each scene; the surroundings, people, their expressions, words, and emotions.

♡ Ask someone what their favourite films are and why they love them. Ask them if they have applied anything from these films into their life or is there anything from these films they would like to apply to their life.

♡ After watching a motion picture with someone or a group of people have a discussion on which bits were your favourites and what you learned. What was the most important message you will take away from the film?

Wise Words

◊ Choose a quote, proverb, saying that resonates with you or a paragraph that you've read and enjoyed from a novel or self-help book. Put aside some time to read and re-read it, then reflect on it word by word. What are the messages you are receiving as you closely and deeply study the paragraph or quote? Let the quote be your quote of the day or even your quote of the week or month. Let the words be your mantra during this period. Delve deeper into the wisdom of the words. Apply its meaning into your day, week, or month. Meditate and put into practice the wisdom of the quotes. There are some great quotes in this book to choose from.

✐ Create a book of your favourite quotes. Perhaps include some of your own quotes. Share the quotes with others.

♡ In a group share thoughts on a quote or paragraph from a book.

♟There are some great films with wonderful quotes, words, and speeches in them. Choose one from a favourite film and delve deeper into its meaning, feelings, and emotions. What do you feel when listening to the words? How does it inspire you? How can you use the sentiment within the words to help you in your life?

♟ Choose a subject, and then look up quotes and sayings related to the subject. Which one resonates with you the most? Put this one into practice.

♡ Remember words of wisdom given to you by a friend, family member, teacher or stranger. In meditation or if possible in person, thank them for their wisdom.

🦋 Make a gift for someone using your favourite words of wisdom. Have a quote printed on a t-shirt. Make a mini-movie using the words. Write a card with the words in it. Write the words on notes and leave them in random places where you or other people can read them. Create a piece of art; write a poem or a song using words of wisdom.

Tree of Gratitude

"Look deeply into the quality of a tree; touch it, feel its solidity, its rough bark, and hear the sound that is part of the tree. Not the sound of wind through the leaves, not the breeze of a morning that flutters the leaves, but its own sound, the sound of the trunk and the silent sound of the roots." Jiddu Krishnamurti

A great way of generating gratitude within ourselves is by doing something creative. Making things with our hands and creating images using colour and shape and texture can free our mind and bring us to a more joyful happier place within ourselves. It takes us back to how we felt when we were children; feeling fully present in the moment, simply enjoying creativity and fun.

Trees are a wonderful symbol of strength and wisdom. They have branches stretching out in many different directions with hundreds of leaves along the branches. They have a solid trunk which holds all the branches together. They have roots that again stretch in many directions underneath the ground. We cannot see these roots but they are very strong and are what holds the whole tree together. We can use the symbol of a tree to make our gratitude practice more creative and fun.

❋ On a piece of wall in your home or in a school classroom if you work as a teacher, stick a large piece of paper directly on the wall or on a board. Draw or paint a trunk, its branches, and its roots. The roots should be the same length going down underneath the ground as the branches are going up over the trunk. Be as creative as you want and make the tree as large as you like, depending on the space you have. Cut out paper circles or droplet shapes which represent raindrops. Cut out paper leaves and fruit shapes which represent the leaves and fruit on the tree, all in different colours, shapes, and sizes and place them in a bowl along with some coloured pens next to the tree.

* On the circle or droplet-shaped paper write down something that you are grateful for from your past and stick them on the roots of the tree. The roots of the tree can represent your ancestors, things that have

happened in the past for which you are grateful, people from your past that you are grateful for, such as teachers, family, and friends or even strangers who have helped you. It could be achievements from your past; it could also be something that didn't go so well in your life that you learned from. You could also write about the gadgets, inventions, inventors, workers, machinery, and processes that have helped you be where you are today.

* On the leaf-shaped paper write down something that you are grateful for now or around you and then stick them on the branches of the tree. It could be what you are doing or have in your life now that you are grateful for – family, friends, health, the Sun, the clouds, trees, your breath, food, mobile, internet, eyes. They can represent qualities that you or others possess, almost anything you are grateful for now.

* The fruit-shaped paper represents the future. What would you be grateful for if it happened to you in the future, what are your goals, dreams, and intentions? What skills and abilities would you like to develop? Stick these on the tree branches. You can write as little or as much as you want. You could create a tree for yourself or with your family or in a school. Gradually you will build a beautiful symbolic tree of gratitude.

❋ *Christmas Tree* – When Christmas comes around, hang decorations of things which symbolise your gratitude. For example, small gifts that you have been given, or that were made for you or things you have made. You could hang things from nature or sentimental things from your family or friends. Little photos in little photo frames. You can collect things of gratitude each year. When you put the tree up each Christmas and hang your decorations you will be reminded of all those things you are grateful for.

❋ Choose a tree in your garden or a tree in nature to hang your messages and symbols of gratitude on. Make something special that represents your gratitude; make it out of material that will be able to withstand different weather conditions. Over time your tree of gratitude will fill up with many symbols of your appreciation.

Pebble in My Hand

Rocks, stones, and pebbles are all made from the Earth's structure when it was formed billions of years ago. They come in a variety of shapes forms and textures. The smoothness of stones and pebbles are created from rocks which are worn away over time by wind, water, the Sun and the movements of our Earth's surface. Each rock, stone, and pebble contains minerals from the Earth and by holding one in our hand we are holding on to our Earth's essence and a story of the creation of our Planet. Each one of them is different, each beautiful in its own way. If you look carefully you will find them everywhere in nature, all formed in their uniquely different way. We can use these lovely small natural pieces of our Earth to help remind us to be grateful.

❋ Choose a rock, stone or pebble, to be your special gratitude symbol, one that you particularly like for its shape, form, colour, texture or sentimental value. Choose one that you can easily carry around with you. You could place the stone in an area where you spend a lot of time, like your car, or kitchen or next to your computer or meditation area. Each time you place your eyes on it, put the stone in your hand and think of something to be grateful for.

❋ Choose a stone which you can share with others in a game of gratitude. With a group of people or children, pass the stone around, each person who has the stone holds it in their hand and has to say something they are grateful for to the rest of the group. The stone gradually contains the energy of gratitude of many people and the feeling of shared gratefulness multiples in each person.

❋ Place the stone in your pocket or your handbag. Every time you put your hand in your pocket or in your handbag you are feeling your gratitude stone and you have to think of something you are grateful for. Look at something within yourself or your environment in that moment. It is a wonderful way of reminding yourself to be grateful for what is here right now. The stone will eventually have even greater value to you as it contains the essence of your positive vibrations of gratefulness.

Just a Little Note to Say...

✒ Make your own little "Thank you" notes using photos, art, colours, your own unique creativity; you may even want to print several notes. The note could simply have the words "Thank You" or "I am Grateful" written on the front, or it could be more detailed. Leave the back of the card blank for you to write a special message on. Make several of these little notes or cards and keep them on you. When you feel like conveying your gratitude to someone give the note to them or you may want to be anonymous so you can leave it somewhere they will see it or find it. It will be a pleasant surprise when they do read it. It's a great way to show your appreciation and brighten someone's day. You can also create your own electronic "Thank you" notes, with pictures or art or a photo and send it via mobile or email to someone. However you want to do it, giving just a little note of thanks is a simple way to express your gratitude to someone. It will most definitely lift the spirits and smiles of everyone involved.

Swept Away

🌍 While you are walking around or sitting in the area in which you live, look around, notice how the area is kept clean, notice the dustbins, feel grateful for those who empty these dustbins. Look at the place you work, someone must be helping to keep it clean. Appreciate the dustbin workers who empty the bins you fill up every week. You could even leave a "Thank you" note for them when they next come to empty your bins or stick a note on the bin "Thank you for emptying our bin, we are very grateful". Help to keep your environment clean by picking up litter when you see it. You can carry a bag around with you and go to a particular area to help pick up litter, wearing gloves or using a tool to help you. Others may see you do this and be encouraged to do the same themselves elsewhere. Many hands make light work – so get your family, friends, and community involved. Get your local council environmental department involved. Your environment will be grateful to you and you will also feel better for your contribution in helping to keep your environment tidier.

Reduce, Reuse & Recycle

To show our appreciation for our environment we can be more mindful of how we manage waste. Think twice before you throw something away. It saves energy and natural resources, helps to reduce pollution and reduces the need for landfills. If everyone did their bit to help, together we can all make a huge difference. When we 'reduce', we conserve – using natural resources wisely, and using less than usual to avoid waste. We can 'reuse' materials in their own original form instead of throwing them away, or pass those materials on to others who could use them. When it comes to 'recycling', simply don't throw away anything that can be recycled. We not only help protect our environment when we practice the three Rs, but we also show our gratitude for the things that we have used and for the way they have helped us. All these items have enhanced our lives in some way and we can but simply show our respect and appreciation to them by reducing, reusing or recycling.

🌍 Reduce

- Almost 4 billion trees are cut down each year for paper use. Recycling 1 tonne of paper saves roughly 31 trees.
- Print or photocopy only when really necessary.
- Use electronic ways of storing information rather than on paper.
- Many products can be bought loose and in less packaging.
- Buy only what you need and use all of what you buy or when you are through with something, pass it along to other people who can continue to put it to good use.
- Reduce how much water you use in your home. Turn the water off when brushing teeth or soaping your hands.
- Switch the lights off in your home or workspace when you don't need them on.
- Switch off electronic devices when not in use.
- Use the car less and walk where you can.
- Use energy-efficient devices such as LED lights which use at least 75% less energy, and last 25 times longer.

✪ Reuse

- Donate unwanted furniture and appliances to charity.
- Pack food in reusable containers rather than foil or cling film.
- Borrow and lend things in your neighbourhood.
- Clean out all your old clothes and donate them to someone in need or a charity shop. Your old is someone else's new.
- If you have a good book you've read that's just sitting around on a bookshelf, give it away to a friend or a charity store.
- Take old carrier bags to the shop with you to use again or use them as bin liners.
- Scrap paper can be used on both sides, for children's drawings and shopping lists. Print on both sides of paper.
- Re-use plastic containers, bottles, and jars.
- Repair broken items, rather than buy new ones.
- Buy reusable products instead of disposable ones, like rechargeable batteries, plastic washable cups, plates or utensils.
- Upcycle – convert old, discarded, unwanted items into something useful.

✪ Recycle

- Recycle cans, plastics, glass bottles, paper, card, metals, electronic equipment, etc.
- Buy products made from recycled material e.g. kitchen/toilet rolls.
- Choose products that come in packaging which you know can be recycled.
- If you can, compost your garden waste and vegetable peelings or take your garden waste to a recycling centre.
- Collect rainwater in a water butt; use it to water your plants.
- Encourage work colleagues to recycle by introducing recycling bins in your workplace.

Share, educate and encourage others to practice the three Rs.

A Prayer of Thanks

"If the only prayer you said in your whole life was, 'thank you', that would suffice." Meister Eckhart

Prayer is simply a conversation from our thoughts and hearts to a higher consciousness or energy. This may be to a god, the universe, life force, the cosmos, the divine, the soul, source, or the higher self or a representation of the higher self or a person who we greatly respect and look up to. We also have these inner conversations with those we love, people in our lives that are living and people who have passed on.

Each one of us whether we realise it or not, pray. Perhaps we don't know to whom or what we are praying to but we certainly all have these conversations in our hearts and minds. We pray for help and guidance, we ask questions to which we hope to receive answers, we pray for others, we wish for things, we pray for strength through difficult times, we are thankful and feel grateful in our prayers, we pray on our own in the silence and we pray in groups.

Praying is a beautiful and humbling way to cultivate gratitude. In silence and in meditation we can truly be ourselves and have a one-to-one conversation with whoever we want or to a beautiful energy that has deep wisdom and will always listen and understand. Having daily conversations of prayer opens our hearts and allows wisdom to flower and gratitude to flow very easily.

🧘 Choose a place that you love spending time in. It could be in your home, a favourite spot in your bedroom or living room; it could be in a beautiful place in nature, a place where you feel at peace and a place where you can sit in silence. Each day sit in this place for five minutes or more and pray. Have a silent conversation from your heart and give thanks. Convey your gratitude for anything that comes into your heart and mind. You can start the conversation with "I am grateful for" or "Thank you for" or "I am thankful for".

You can place symbols in front of you to help you pray, such as a candle or something from nature or a photo of someone you love and respect.

&⃯ In our prayers, we can also ask for guidance for cultivating gratitude within ourselves. If we find we are struggling with being grateful for something or someone or a situation, ask for a way to look for the gratitude within it, ask for a way to turn your perceptions and attitudes around into something more positive. You will find that wisdom comes through to give you guidance and your mind and heart will feel more at ease.

♡ You may like to gather a group of friends together or a community to meditate and pray with. Each time you all meet, a person within the group suggests a subject to pray or meditate about or a person to pray for. Everyone sits in silence and prays on the subject or the person for about ten minutes. At the end, if people would like to, they can share what they experienced or learned from their prayer.

&⃯ Prayer doesn't have to be where there is silence. You can pray at any time during your day, in any environment, it any situation, especially in difficult situations, prayer can be very powerful. We are constantly having conversations in our minds through thoughts and in our hearts and body through feelings. Prayer is a way of directing those thoughts and feelings into grateful ones, to ask questions to which we receive wise guidance, to gain strength to overcome adversity, to see the positive. Whoever or whatever we are speaking to will give us the wisdom to know for ourselves what we need to think, feel and do. Ask a question in your prayer or meditation – wait and listen to the guidance and wisdom you receive back.

◊ Prayer flags in the Tibetan tradition carry messages of peace, strength, compassion, and wisdom upon the wind to all people. Create your own prayer flag and hang it outside so that it carries your message upon the wind. You can write a prayer on a piece of paper and place it somewhere in nature or make something special to represent your prayer.

Gratitude Sharing

"A joy that's shared is a joy made double." English Proverb

When other's voice their thoughts it can open our mind to a different perspective. We are able to see things from a different point of view. When we share our thoughts we connect our minds and hearts with others. Sharing positive thoughts has a ripple effect; the essence of the thought continues onto others which then continue on to even more people. So by sharing a positive thought with one person, you are also sharing it with many more people whom you have never met. A positive thought, word or action continues on in many ways and in many different directions, just like the light from a star travels in all directions and reaches our awareness millions of years after it has been emitted. Sharing what we are grateful for with someone else passes on that gratitude. Your gratitude becomes part of someone else and they will feel the essence of your appreciation. When we work together with a group of people, many minds, many thoughts and ideas join together to create a collective consciousness which can change and enhance our way of seeing things.

♡ Share your gratitude in the middle of a conversation with someone you know, say something positive and uplifting. When sharing your gratitude you may also want to delve deeper and explain why you are grateful for it, elaborating further increases the feeling and understanding behind what you are grateful for.

♡ While having a meal around a table with your family or friends at home or eating out, ask everyone to share something they are grateful for; it could be from their day or any other gratitude. This is a great practice to do with children while you are having your meal together. It is a beautiful way to connect while sharing a meal.

♡ Choose someone special in your life; it could be a partner, a family member, a friend or a work colleague and team up with them to share gratitude with each other. Each day share one gratitude each. One gratitude becomes two each day.

♡ While doing an activity together with someone, share your gratitude for things that are around you at that moment, ask them to share also. By sharing this way you increase your gratitude for what you are doing and for what is around you.

♡ Play a gratitude sharing game. For example – two teams; one member of the team takes it in turns to give gratitude clues about something written on a piece of paper that they have randomly picked from a hat. Then the other team members have to guess what it is.

♡ Sometimes we get so used to things in our life that we stop feeling appreciation for them. Experience things, people, places you love through the eyes of another, share something you love with another person, giving you a fresh outlook and rekindling your appreciation for those things.

♡ Gather together a group of people, (3 or more people); you could all sit in a circle if you choose. Think of something that all of you can practice gratitude on. You could place an item or a symbol or a picture of the item in the middle, or pass the item/symbol/picture around the group. One by one each person in the group shares their positive feelings of gratitude on the item or subject. The subject could be a place that you have all been to or a person that you all know or something in your environment, in your home, something that we all use on a regular basis. This practice has a snowball effect, starting out small and slowly gaining more and more volume and value as it rolls on. With each person's gratitude being expressed, everyone's appreciation grows and grows until by the end you have a huge ball of gratitude shared amongst everyone.

♡ Technology has made different forms of communication easier through email and mobile chat applications. Start a group gratitude discussion amongst friends or family. Each person in the group at a time thinks of a subject for everyone to share their positive feelings and gratitude on. A picture of the subject matter can be sent to all the people in the group and then each one can express their grateful feelings with everyone else in the group.

I Wish You Well

Many people carry around resentments and hurt from the past towards someone or a group of people or day-to-day anger towards people and situations they come across. Sometimes we can be hurt by something someone did or didn't do or because they weren't there for us during a time of need. The reasons can be many for holding ill will towards another. Holding onto resentments and anger only creates more pain inside ourselves and can have a negative rippling effect on those around us. This kind of resentment can feel like an illness in our body, slowly reducing our energy and affecting our health, stability, and spirit. Whenever we have an illness of resentment we need to try and understand the roots of why we feel this way. We need to look very deeply at the other person and why they may have hurt us and look deep inside ourselves to find why we are holding onto anger and resentment. When we can understand others and ourselves more deeply we will begin to be able to transform and dissolve the bad feelings inside ourselves and replace them with feelings of love and well wishes.

Changing our own internal response and attitude towards those who have hurt us will free our mind and heart and allow our spirit to grow. A great way to generate goodwill and positive thoughts towards others and to release or dissolve any resentment within yourself is to wish everyone wellness, good health, happiness and peace within your heart. In Hindu culture, they say "Om Shanti" which means "I am a peaceful soul and I wish you peace". In Buddhism, they say "A lotus for you", a gesture of peace and wisdom. In Christianity, they say "God bless you". However long you've been holding ill feelings inside yourself let it go and replace it with a feeling of goodwill. It could be a quick thought in your mind of peace and love or a much deeper prayer of good wishes. This may not sound easy, but it is a simple change in our perception and attitude. Every time you do this it will get easier and more natural. In time you will begin to respond naturally. It will slowly become your nature and way of being, and others around you will see and feel the benefit of your positive attitude and energy. By wishing others well, you are in turn wishing yourself well.

♡ A lot of the time resentments can come out of misunderstanding. Try and see a situation from the other person's point of view. Acknowledge that everyone has their own difficulties and sufferings that make them act in certain ways. If a person has hurt you in some way, imagine yourself in their shoes, transport yourself in your mind into their life, into their surroundings, look deeply at their past, their childhood, the conditions surrounding them and the people they are surrounded by and try to understand how they live and perceive those around them. Through this deeper understanding of them, you will be able to help dissolve the anger and resentment in your heart towards them and to send them good wishes, in meditation, prayer or in person.

♡ See all the people in your life that have hurt you as your greatest teachers. Teachers who have brought you to a place where you need to learn to understand deeply. Feel grateful for all the lessons that they have taught you. If we did not have these lessons in our lives how would we ever learn to be more understanding and practice peace? If everything went well in our lives where is the growth in our spirit? So be grateful for all the lessons and wish them well.

♡ For those who you loved, but are no longer in your life, those who had upset you in some way; feel grateful that they were part of your life and that you loved them. Send them your blessings and loving prayers and wish them well wherever they are.

♡ There is a beautiful meditation from the Buddhist tradition called "The Loving Kindness Meditation". It allows you to send kindness and well wishes firstly towards yourself, then a person you are close to, then a person you have neutral feelings towards, then a person you have difficulty with and finally the whole world. There are many versions of this meditation to choose from online. Practising this meditation on a regular basis will most certainly expand and open your heart. Allow the love that already resides within you to shine out towards everyone around you.

◉ Imagine a glow of coloured light beaming from the centre of your heart into the whole of your body wishing you well and beaming outside your body wishing everything and everyone around you well.

Heartfulness

"The heart is a thousand stringed instrument, that can only be tuned with love." Hafiz

"All you need is Love", a well known Beatles song says it all. When we feel love whether it's given or received, we generally feel the sensation of love generated in the physical area of our heart. We physically can feel our heart expanding. The heart has been considered the source of emotion and wisdom for centuries. Much research has been done by the HeartMath Institute to explain the scientific connection between the heart and mind. Our heart has a deep connection with the hearts of others; we can sense vibrations from the heart area, an intuitive knowing. Studies have shown that the heart picks up intuitive information prior to the brain.

The heart has a system of neurons that have both short-term and long-term memory, and their signals sent to the brain can affect our emotional experiences. The heart sends more information to the brain than vice versa. It emits electromagnetic fields that change according to our emotions. This magnetic field or vibrations can be measured up to several feet away from the body. The vibrations of emotions that are generated in the heart interact with the heart vibrations of those around us, it almost acts as a second mind with its own sense of awareness; it has its own consciousness and affects the way we perceive our world. When we feel positive emotions like gratitude, love, inspiration, joy, and appreciation, the heart beats out a certain message. Because the heart radiates out the largest electromagnetic field in the body, we can have an impact on those around us as we are fundamentally and deeply connected with each other and the Planet itself. We can feel more confidence and trust in our intuition knowing that it's the intelligence of the heart continuously scanning the future for us, guiding and protecting us. So trust your vibes, as it's sensing the energetic fields around you. Trust the feelings and experiences you have inside your heart centre and allow yourself to fully feel and connect with whatever it is that arises within it.

♡ Heart Breath — Focus your awareness in the area of your heart, the centre of your chest. Keeping your awareness here, imagine you are breathing from your heart centre — breathing deeply in and out through your heart. The air flowing into your heart as you breathe in, and out of the area of your heart as you breathe out. As you continue breathing in this way, generate a genuine feeling of love, compassion, care, gratitude, joy, appreciation for someone or something in your life. This will activate your heart and send positive emotions throughout your entire body, raising your vibrations and creating an abundant positive, loving and grateful energy field around you.

♡ Your heart has spoken to you all your life and will continue to do so. Think of a time that you followed your heart's guidance and it turned out well. Think of a time when you didn't follow your heart's intuition but followed the thoughts that came rushing into your mind suppressing the heart's messages and it didn't turn out well. Trust your heart's intuitive intelligence. Become aware of your feelings and trust them as inner guidance that ushers you through life, rather than trying to suppress this inner wisdom. Ask your heart for guidance when you need it. Calm the mind and emotions and listen for the first thought that comes to you that feels right. Follow your heart and see what happens. Ask questions to your heart, usually, it's the first instant response that comes back to you that is the right one.

♡ Generating positive feelings within ourselves emits powerful vibrations from the heart centre to the area surrounding us. Notice how you feel when you are with someone who is positive, especially when you have been quite low. Notice how they helped change the vibration in your heart to an uplifted one. Notice how feeling grateful suddenly uplifts you. What are the sensations you feel in your heart centre? Notice when you express your gratitude to someone, how their energy, expression, vibration changes for the better. Your elevated vibration flows from one heart to another. A large group of people producing heart coherence can have a huge impact on the world.

♡ Place your hand on your chest, over your heart centre, allowing the beautiful emotions that flow from within it to be experienced and felt deeply.

Speak from Your Heart

"Gratitude is not only the greatest of virtues but the parent of all the others." Cicero

Words, when spoken, are our thoughts expressed through our mind from our body into the atmosphere and listened to by ourselves and others. We can speak in the privacy of our own home, in a sacred space created by ourselves, in nature where we are alone. Our minds think thousands of thoughts per day. By feeling gratitude and then expressing it through spoken words you are separating it from all the other thoughts running around in your mind and increasing the gratitude that you feel, affirming your gratefulness to yourself and the universe.

♡ Create a sacred space in your home. It could be a room or a certain part of a room. Place pictures or flowers or light a candle, anything that is special to you and helps you feel peaceful. You could also create a space in your garden, or find a place in nature which is special to you. While you are in this space speak or whisper what you are grateful for. Choose things from the day that you are grateful for, or someone you are grateful for and say why. When you speak the words, you start to find the difference between what is a thought that is constantly running through your mind and what you are actually saying, the power of our words are very important. Saying "I am grateful for" out loud can create a change in your heart and mind.

♡ When you are on your own, speak openly and express your gratitude to someone you know or have known. They may be still part of your life or have moved away or passed away. Express your thanks to them. They can sense and hear you from wherever they are as we are all interconnected by vibrations of energy.

♡ When you are on your own, speak out loud words of gratitude for dreams you'd like to experience. Express your gratitude for them as if they are already happening or already happened. Look forward to them. Generate words and feelings of joy and excitement.

♡ Use an audio recorder to record your gratitude. Smart mobile phones have free audio recording apps on them or you could purchase an audio recorder. Each day speak your words of thanks for something and record it. This is a wonderful way of preserving your spoken words. After recording you can give it a title and then whenever you need reminding of your gratitude or you are feeling low and need reminding of something good you can listen again to how you felt about the people, things, experiences that you are grateful for.

♡ Record messages to yourself reminding you to be more grateful for certain things. Perhaps there is something in particular you want to work on within yourself, allow your own recorded voice and words of wisdom to teach you gratitude.

♫ Sing a song or recite a poem of gratitude, either one written by yourself or by someone else. You can either sing the song or recite the poem to yourself, to someone else or record it and give it to someone you care about as a gift.

♡ Record your spoken words of gratitude and send it to someone special or to someone who really needs to hear it. The message could be about them or something else relating to gratitude. Send it via your mobile phone, or give them the message as mp3 or on a CD. It would make a lovely surprise gift message.

♡ When you are on your own somewhere, where no one can hear you but yourself, speak your gratefulness to something that is around you, tell this something whatever it may be how grateful you are to it. It could be your food, an object, something in the environment, a feeling, an attitude, an experience.

♡ Express grateful words to yourself using any of the methods in this section. Through spoken words, songs, poems, recorded, in a private sacred place. Say 'Thank you' to yourself every day for something about yourself that has helped you. You can even speak words of appreciation to someone else about yourself like "I appreciate that I ....","I am grateful to myself for....", "I felt I did so well when I....".

Meaningful Conversations

"To listen well is as powerful a means of influence as to talk well, and is as essential to all true conversation." Chinese Proverb

Having more meaningful conversations and learning about the other person gives us a chance to learn so much more about someone's life story. It can touch something within ourselves and we go away learning something about ourselves as well as the other person and that's something truly to be grateful for. Psychological research studies have shown that more meaningful conversations can actually lead to increased levels of happiness and wellbeing, not necessarily because the content of the conversation is of a more positive nature but because deeper conversations help us find more meaning and importance in our own lives. Everyone has an amazing story to tell, each of these stories carries life lessons, experiences, and wisdom that we can learn from. Practice mindful deep listening. See where the conversation takes you. Make eye contact. Try and really see the person you are talking to; their expressions, mannerisms, and the way they are interacting with you. Here are some questions to start you off.

- What qualities do you value and appreciate in another?
- What would you like to do before you pass away?
- Which person (alive or passed away) would you love to have a conversation with and what one question would you ask them?
- What is your favourite childhood memory?
- Which of your dreams is at the top of your list?
- Who or what has inspired you most in your life and why?
- What new habit do you want to instil in yourself and why?
- What do you most admire about yourself?
- What gives you the greatest joy and why?
- Which country would you love to visit and why?
- Describe something you achieved that you didn't think was possible?
- What life advice would you offer a newborn infant?
- What advice would you offer yourself 5 years ago? 1 year ago? Today?
- How would you most like to be remembered?

♡ When you have had a more meaningful conversation with someone or a group of people ask yourself what have I learned from it? How has it helped me?

Gadgets, Gizmos, and Tools

"All the tools and engines on earth are only extensions of man's limbs and senses." Ralph Waldo Emerson

We all benefit from gadgets and tools in our lives. Some of these include technical gadgets such as televisions, remote controls, phones, digital cameras, computers, laptops, tablets, mp3 players, DVD players. Others include gadgets and tools in the kitchen such as knives, cutting boards, pots and pans, spoons and forks, blenders, refrigerators, kettles, microwaves. Some help with DIY such as screwdrivers, drills, lawnmowers, garden cutters, forks, and spades. The list goes on. All gadgets make our life easier, more enjoyable and much more convenient. Allow yourself to feel gratitude and appreciation for the gadgets and tools in your life.

♡ There are so many people and materials that make it possible for these gadgets and tools to be in your life. From the person or people who invented the gadgets and tools to all the materials that it took to make them. From the people who helped make it in a factory to the machinery that allowed it to be made. From the transport by car, lorry, ship or plane to the people who used this transport to bring it into your life. Choose a gadget or tool that you use. Look deeply at it and think of all the ways it helps you, how it makes your life easier or more enjoyable. What does it allow you to achieve, what does it teaches you? Then think of all the people and materials that were involved in bringing it into your life. How was it made? Generate the deep feelings of gratitude while using the gadget, making sure you take good care of it and that it continues to be well looked after.

♡ Perhaps you'd like to speak out loud your feelings of appreciation for the gadget. Saying a few words on why you are grateful to it. Talk to others about how grateful you are for the wonderful gadgets around you, encouraging them to do the same. Ask them to choose a gadget or tool, and then explain why they are grateful for it, giving an example of how it's helped them.

Have you tried turning it off and on again?

As long as people have been around, information technology has been around because there have always been ways of communicating through technology. When humans started communicating they would use language or simple picture drawings usually carved on a rock. People then developed writing tools and the abacus as a calculator. Then came mechanical computers, the telegraph, and the telephone system. Now we have the digital computer which has brought us into the world of the internet and mobile technology.

Computer technology has greatly enhanced how we can communicate with each other. We can be so grateful for the knowledge we accumulate from sharing information with each other. We have access to infinite amounts of free information, advice, learning from many people around the world through the many tools such as computers, mobiles, and tablets. They enable us to connect with other people and to stay in touch with friends and family members from anywhere on the Planet. They give us pleasure, exercise the mind, help us achieve our goals and are a means by which many people earn their living.

🧘 When using a computer, tablet, mobile or any other information or computer technology tool, give thanks to the unseen hands and minds that helped create the amazing machine.

✏️ Type a thank you message from yourself to your machine using your machine, save it somewhere on your machine. Write down the many ways your machine has helped you, what you enjoy most about using it, what your favourite part about it is, perhaps a particular application, thank it for helping you to connect with people you care about, mention someone in particular that it helps you connect with and how grateful you are for it.

♡ Talk with other people and share with each other about how grateful you are for computer technology and pick out something specific about it that has helped you and talk about it in more detail.

♡ Sometimes we can get frustrated with our machines when they stop working well. The simple solution from most might be "have you tried turning it off and on again?". Most of the time this gets it working again. Be patient with your machine, sometimes all it needs is a refresh and reboot.

✎ Stick a "Thank you" sticky note or "Thank you" card on your machine – somewhere on your computer, on the inside of your mobile cover or tablet cover so you see it when you open the case.

♡ If you've learned something from an internet site and if the internet site has an email address or a response section, send a "Thank you" message to the people who set up the internet site or respond gratefully to someone who posted something online that has helped you.

☺ It is important to have a balanced relationship with technology. So give yourself plenty of breaks and space away from technology and when you do come back to using it you are fresher, more focused, mindful and more appreciative of how it helps you.

⚓ Think about a time in your life in the past where technology was very different, not so advanced as it is now but still as amazing to you at the time. Look back and smile at how you felt about the newest technology in your past. Think of an item now, how did you feel when you first used it? Generate thankful feelings for it again. Exchange past technology stories and experiences with others.

⚓ Delve into future technological changes that you'd like to see develop, something that you know will most likely happen or think up some more inventive ideas that may seem farfetched but would love to see developed. Think of all the benefits to mankind through the new technology, look forward to experiencing it and send your gratitude for it into the future.

⚓ See how many items in a day you can spot that require some form of computer technology to allow them to function. With each item you notice ask yourself 'how does it help me in my life or the lives of others?'

◊ Set an alarm on a device to remind you to be grateful for technology.

Replacing an Ungrateful Thought

"All action results from thought, so it is thoughts that matter." Sai Baba

When we have ungrateful thoughts during the day, unpleasant feelings can be created within us, which can lead to stress and resentment. It can soon become a habit that affects our lives, our health, and our relationships.

Our ungrateful thoughts can be about many things. They can be about the weather, the traffic, our jobs, our family, and friends, about someone who has done something or said something which we did not agree with, it could be about food, it could be about the bills or doing something you don't want to do.

Learning to be more mindful of our ungrateful thoughts is a practice which can transform us and change our lives. Everyone has negative thoughts, the important thing is to acknowledge and replace these thoughts with grateful positive thoughts. This way the ungrateful thought is dissolved by gratitude. You could almost be grateful for the ungrateful thought because without having this thought you would not be practising to be more grateful. You will find through this practice more appreciation and value for what you were originally ungrateful for.

It doesn't matter if the ungrateful thought is replaced immediately or much later. Becoming aware of the thought and transforming it at any time into a positive eventually creates a change in our way of thinking and perceiving. When our way of thinking is more grateful and appreciative our life begins to change for the better. Our minds and hearts become lighter and freer. We begin to see everything that happens as an opportunity for inner change and transformation.

The more we practice becoming aware of our ungrateful thoughts and the negative words spoken by others, we no longer go along with these thoughts and accept them as truth. We will automatically start to replace the ungrateful thoughts with something more positive until eventually, our thoughts in the main are naturally grateful. We are gradually able to handle life's challenges with more stability.

⚘ During the course of a day watch out for ungrateful negative thoughts that pop into your mind. Without placing any judgment on the thought look within yourself, find an alternative perspective, change your interpretation and turn it around to something positive.

⚘ Watch out for the negative thoughts on things, people, and situations that we have no control over such as the weather, the traffic, things that people say and do. We need to understand that we have no control over these things, and find an alternative interpretation.

⚘ Through an ungrateful thought, there may be something that we can learn from or something that we need to increase our appreciation for.

♡ If we hear someone verbalise their ungrateful thought, say something to turn it around, into something more positive. Show them a different perspective, one which is grateful.

⚘ Looking even deeper we may try to find the root of our ungrateful thought, it may be nothing to do with the person or situation. Look at it as a deeper practice to finding the root of your negativity to a particular person or situation. Think of something or someone now that you are finding hard to be grateful for. Close your eyes. Ask yourself why am I feeling this way? Why do I have this negative opinion? Just as a tree has many roots, travel down one of the roots and see where your self-inquiry takes you. This helps dissolve the ungrateful thought or feeling, replacing it with a deeper understanding of yourself, the other person, the situation or the experience.

♡ If someone says something hurtful, critical, ungrateful or negative to you or about you, replace it in your own mind and heart to something grateful, uplifting and positive about yourself. Rather than take other people's negative comments to heart, form a deeper understanding of where these comments stem from and at the same time value yourself.

A Room with a View

"Be the change you wish to see in the world." Mahatma Gandhi

Imagine you are in a room with a window, if you looked through the window the view from it of the outside would be from the perspective of the window you are looking out of. If you were in another room in another part of the building your view would be different, the view would be from the perspective of that room, but the outside is the same, it is just being seen from two different angles, two different points of view, and two different perspectives. We interpret, perceive, what we are looking at through the window we are standing in front of. Our body is like the room and our mind's eye the window. We all see and feel differently according to own perspectives, our own perceptions, based on where we are in life, our life experiences, our conditions, our culture, what we have learned, our background, our influences, our attitudes, and our mood.

Many arguments and disagreements can arise from different opinions and somehow we feel that we are right and the other is wrong, but neither is right or wrong, we just see things from a different perspective. We are all individual and have our own points of view.

Our perspective and perceptions can change from moment to moment, our mind is very fluid. One moment we may think and see things a certain way, the next moment we may think completely differently. Sometimes someone shares their point of view and we begin to see things from a fresh new perspective. Sometimes we can become so fixed in our points of view it is very hard to change, but if we keep our minds and hearts open we come to understand that the world is more beautiful because we are all different and learning to see from other people's perspectives can open up a whole new world to us; the world seems bigger and a more wondrous place. If we took away all the rooms and we all saw the world through a three-dimensional window, there would be countless possible ways of seeing and perceiving any given situation and the world around us.

🧘 Looking at things in hindsight is one of life's blessings. Think back to a challenging time in your life. Try and remember how you perceived the situation back then, how did you feel about it, what were your thoughts? How differently do you feel now looking back in perspective, looking back through a different window of the present moment? Your interpretation of the experience could now be completely different. Be grateful when you manage to look at a situation differently. You may be able to see the benefits of what happened in the past when at the time you could not. Experiencing painful growth creates the greatest shifts in our perceptions.

♡ When you are with someone observing something together, allow the other person to express their perspective and their perceptions of what you are observing. Be grateful for their opinion, be respectful of their views. By showing that you are open to see things differently, they will be more willing to learn to be open to your points of view too and you can both learn from each other. This applies to group opinions as well. You may be seeing things from a negative perspective, but the other person may see something positive within it, be grateful for when they help you see things optimistically. Thank them for shining a different light onto a subject. You can also lift someone out of their negative perceptions into a more balanced view.

☺ It has been shown that our perceptions and beliefs, our interpretation of our environment has an impact on our biology, chemistry and gene expression. Our bodies adapt to our environment, but our environment is how we choose to see it. If we choose to see our environment in a negative light, our body and life shift to create more negativity. If we choose to perceive the world through a more positive light, our body and life will express the biology, chemistry and DNA expression that will most benefit us. You are rewriting the chemistry of your body every time you change your perception. Start small and notice some of your negative views about yourself, other people and your world. Open your mind and heart, what is it now saying to you? Alter your perceptions to something more positive or balanced.

An Attitude of Gratitude

"I am convinced that life is 10% what happens to me and 90% how I react to it. And so it is with you, we are in charge of our attitudes."
Charles R. Swindoll

Our state of mind or frame of mind, mindset or disposition can affect our outlook, the way we perceive our lives and the world around us. Our attitude influences our opinions on people, situations, and experiences and affects how we approach something.

🧘 Think of a time in the past in which you approached a challenging situation with a positive state of mind. Your attitude helped you, it may have also helped someone else or those around you too. How would you describe your attitude? It could have been wise, balanced, peaceful, joyful, optimistic, non-judgemental. Feel grateful for your attitude in this situation.

♡ Acknowledge and be grateful for a particularly good mood or a positive state of mind that you are in and for sharing it with others. Positive and uplifting states of mind such as happiness, joy, freedom, safety, love, peace, wisdom, inspiration, excitement, calmness.

♡ Be grateful for someone else's attitude. Perhaps someone you know has a positive outlook on life which helps you see things in a different light. Someone's good mood may have lifted your mood or someone else may have approached a situation from a different frame of mind which you appreciate.

♡ You find yourself in a not-so-good state of mind, you are in a bad mood, your attitude towards something is not helping you, you are judgmental and critical and it is all making you more stressed and winding you up and possibly winding up those around you even more. You are worried about something, you're feeling negative and at the moment you are not feeling happy at all. Perhaps you feel bad about how you approached something that happened and you wish you'd approached it differently. The first thing to do is to become mindful of how you are feeling, acknowledge it and say to yourself "I am here for you". Say to yourself, "I understand that you are not in a good place inside your head and heart but we must do our best to try and change this mindset to a more positive one". Be grateful that you noticed and acknowledged your not-so-good state of mind as you can now change it. Put your hand on your heart, breathe deeply and send yourself a lot of love, compassion, and understanding. In your mind speak to yourself gently with loving kind words. Gently guide yourself to a new perspective by tapping into your own innate wisdom and the wonderful qualities that you possess. Be grateful for being able to settle your mind and heart down, changing your frame of mind to a calm and positive state.

When you find yourself engaging in a negative conversation about something, ask yourself what can I do to help this situation? Is my complaining about it helping? What attitude will help this situation?

Have you ever noticed that when something goes wrong we can't understand why it happened and then complain about it or we get angry and frustrated and then we tell other people what went wrong. What about the hundreds of things that went right, what about all the blessings that are right under our nose all the time. Let's become more aware of those and talk about them to other people. If we have an attitude of gratitude we will not make such a mountain of a molehill every time something doesn't go as we'd like it to. The balance is greatly tipping in our favour when it comes to things going right and even when things go wrong seeing it as an opportunity for spiritual growth means that it also is a positive gain in our life. So next time something goes wrong, turn it into a right. There is something right about it if you look deeply enough.

If you recognise a negative attitude towards something you'd like to change, first of all, be grateful to yourself for wanting to change it, and then ask yourself gently why you feel this way about it. With every answer delve even deeper and ask why that is. You may want to write down your answers or do this in meditation. Then ask yourself what attitude would you like to adopt? How would you like to feel about it? Do this daily and notice the shift in your attitude; in your thoughts, feelings, and actions.

Believe or Not to Believe

"The only person you are destined to become is the person you decide to be." Ralph Waldo Emerson

A belief is an assumption or conviction held to be true either by an individual or a group, regarding concepts, events, people and things. We acquire most of our beliefs from childhood, from our family, our teachers, our surroundings, our environment, our culture, our society, what we see and hear and what we learn through life. But are any of these beliefs really true or are they just thoughts, feelings and opinions of the people and world around us which we have chosen to believe as truth?

Sometimes we adopt or take on the beliefs of others and make them our own so we can feel like we belong or they help to protect us or we hold onto them due to a fear of being different. Sometimes we are taken over by the beliefs of others and we don't even know our own thoughts and feelings, we don't know what is really true for us.

Everyone has their own belief system. What may be true for one person may not be true for another person. Every individual chooses their beliefs. Our beliefs create our reality; they direct our lives in a particular direction. We have beliefs about ourselves, other people, nations, the environment, social beliefs, and cultural beliefs. Many people hold onto a belief because they have been told it is true by people they think they can trust. Typically a person will choose to hold their personal belief until they are provided with evidence to the contrary.

So many beliefs that we hold do not serve us and the world around us, they narrow our minds and hearts and stop us from truly being ourselves. Most of the time we don't even know that we are holding on to beliefs that are not very positive, beliefs which cause us stress and dis-ease and also hinder our relationships and a positive progress through life. Beliefs can help us or hinder us. Let us dive deeply into them to discover what lies within.

♨ Most of the time we think and feel on a subconscious level, so we don't know or understand what our thoughts and beliefs are. 95 percent of our thoughts and beliefs are stored in the subconscious part of our brain, meaning it is programmed to carry out thoughts, patterns, and functions that are automatic. The other 5 percent is our conscious mind, where we make decisions and are more aware and creative. Our mindfulness comes from this part of our mind. The best way to tap into our subconscious programmes of thoughts and beliefs is to start to question them. Start with a belief that you have and dissect it into smaller parts and thoughts you have on the subject.

♨ On a large piece of paper write down a belief that you hold – *My Thoughts/Beliefs on ......* Take some time and make a list and write down all your thoughts about this subject. Everything you feel about it, all your beliefs on the subject. Then look at how many are positive and how many are negative. Ask yourself "Is this a positive thought or belief?", "is this thought or belief helping me?", "Is this thought or belief helping others?", if they are not, then change your perspective and change them into positive thoughts, change them into thoughts that help you or someone else, thoughts that generate and encourage gratitude; slowly you will find your own truth. Take a belief you hold about yourself which you know is not positive. Delve deeply into it to discover the roots of this belief, ask your true self what the truth is, it should be something much kinder and loving towards yourself.

♨ Our beliefs shape our perceptions, our perceptions then drive our thoughts, these then create our attitudes, which generates our feelings and emotions, which fuel our actions, reactions, and behaviours. These create our habits which ultimately shape our character. Start by deeply looking, becoming aware of a part of your character, or a habit that you wish to change. Start to notice your actions, reactions, and behaviours relating to this habit. Become aware of how it makes you feel, or the feelings and emotions behind your behaviour; start to notice how these are shaped by certain thought patterns, attitudes, and perceptions. You will eventually find the belief that is behind it all.

A Warm Thanks

How wonderful it is to feel the warmth on our skin on a lovely sunny day and how comforting it is to have a home that can be heated on a cold winter's day and a car that can be heated to keep us warm on a cold day while driving. Heat helps to warm our water up for washing our dishes and helps us relax and heat up our bodies from soothing hot baths and showers. The heat from the fire produced by our stove and oven helps cook our food, and through thermoelectric generators and the Sun's rays, heat can produce electricity which in itself provides us with a multitude of benefits. Let us appreciate the power of heat and all the factors which help create the heat that we benefit from every day.

☺ When taking a bath or a shower, notice the warmth on your skin from the water. How does the warm water feel on your skin? How do your muscles feel from the heat of the water? Imagine the warm water of Mother Earth blessing your whole body, mind, and spirit with healing and loving energy.

☺ On a cold day when you are in your home and the heating is turned up to keep you warm, become mindful of the position you are in compared to being outside. Be grateful for your heating system, the radiators, the fuel line that comes into your home, the people who installed it all, the fossil fuels like coal and oil that were formed hundreds of millions of years ago underground and under the ocean. Be grateful to Mother Earth for producing the gas and for humans to bring it into your home all helping to keep you warm.

💧 Practice washing up meditation and appreciate the warmth of the water as it helps you wash your pots clean.

🍎 Practice cooking meditation; grateful for the fuel that is helping you to cook your meals, and heat your food. How does it feel when you have a warm, cooked meal especially in the colder seasons?

☺ Give thanks for all your clothes which keep you warm on cold days.

Electric Dreams

It was in 1800 that the first electric battery was invented and it wasn't too long ago in 1879 that the light bulb was invented. Since then our whole world has been illuminated by electric lights. The darkness is filled with light just by a flick of a switch.

Electricity helps to run most of the devices that we use in our home such as washing machines, dryers, kitchen appliances, electric ovens, computers, TVs, mobiles, electric toothbrushes, DIY tools. Our roads are lit up by electricity so we can see where we are driving. Electricity is needed for the machinery used for building work. Many factories could not run without electricity; virtually most of the things we use need electricity to be made.

⚲ Look around you at this very moment. It's very likely that there is something that is run by electricity; is it a lamp, a computer, a street light? Concentrate on one of those items and think of all the ways in which it helps you in your life.

✏ Choose an item in your home that runs on electricity, and stick a "Thank you" sticky note on it. Showing gratitude not only for the item but also the electricity that is needed to run the item. You can extend your gratitude to all the people who helped make the item, to get the item to your home, the power plant and electric cables that bring the electricity into your home, even the inventors of electricity. Perhaps you'd like to leave the sticky note on the item for several days so when you look at it you are reminded of how grateful you are for it.

◗ To show your appreciation for electricity, have a "No Electricity Day". Try to go a whole day without using electricity. In your home, you can use torches or candles, keep your TV and computer off, don't use your mobile as they use electricity to be charged. There's no need to turn electrical items, such as fridges and freezers off, just don't use them. Imagine you had a power cut and you have no choice but to do without electricity. Find other more inventive ways of getting by for just one day.

Home Sweet Home

"There is nothing like staying at home for real comfort." Jane Austen

We each have a place in which we live and call our home. Whether it is a house or an apartment or a room, whether we live on our own or share with others, whether we own your home or rent it, it is a place which is very special to us, a place which is always there for us and provides us with great comfort. Our home keeps us sheltered and protects us from all kinds of weather. It keeps us warm in the colder months and cooler in the warmer months. It is a place to lay our heads down to rest and sleep. Our home allows us to cook our meals, to sit and eat and is a place to wash ourselves. It is a place where we can be on our own or together with our family and friends and enjoy the things we want to do.

🌐 We should regard our home as a sacred place and by looking after it we are expressing our love and gratitude. When you do any housework enjoy the work you do. Do it with a sense of joy and delight. Keep your feelings light and happy. While you are working become more mindful of what you are doing and feel grateful for your home and think of how well you are looking after it. While you are cleaning your home consider each room and how you feel about it, look deeply at what you are cleaning and then see how each item helps you in your daily life and feel grateful for them.

❋ If you have a garden, it is an extension of your home, providing a place for you to interact with nature. Develop a relationship with the trees, plants, and flowers in your garden. They can feel your energy of love, for which they are grateful. Send gratitude to your garden for the beautiful energy of love that it conveys to you in every moment you spend within it. The wildlife and insects that share the lovely space you have created and look after so well will also feel your love and be incredibly grateful to you.

◐ Give your home a name. Perform your own personal ceremony or ritual for your home or a particular room to express your gratitude.

Love of Land and Country

The country in which we live in is an important part of who we are. Whether we were born in the country we live in or emigrated, it has provided us with everything we need to live our lives. Look at all the wonderful things and opportunities your country and the people within it provide you with. It provides you with a home, protection; you've benefited from the food that grows on its land, its education system, all the services it provides, its health service; it provides you with a job to earn a living so you are able to look after yourself and look after your family. Look at its natural world and wildlife, its cultural traditions; every country has its wonder and fascination.

♡ Talk to others about what you particularly appreciate about the country you live in or about a particular region of the country you live in. Encourage others who live in the same country or region to share their own positive views.

♡ If you have lived in other countries, perhaps you were born in another country, learn more about your cultural origins, feel grateful that you have another country to be grateful to for helping you become the person you are today. Share with others all the positives about the country you were born, raised, or have lived in previously.

♡ Ask someone from another country or cultural background what they appreciate about the country they live in or grew up in. This allows us to gain deeper insights into how people live, their culture and traditions and learn about the positive aspects of another country.

♡ Get together a group of people from many different areas around the country you live in and/or many different countries, with many different backgrounds and cultures. Sit in a circle and one by one share something wonderful about the place in which you live or have lived in. What do you appreciate about your cultural background?

◊ Create a ceremony or ritual to celebrate the love for your country.

The Value of Money

At the dawn of humanity, bartering was used in lieu of money to exchange goods and services for other goods and services. As far back as 9000BC, early man would barter goods they had in surplus for ones they lacked. Grain, vegetables, sheep, and cattle were popular goods to barter. Importance was placed on the value of the goods given and received and what was needed to survive.

The first coins were created around 600BC. Coins then evolved into bank notes around 1661AD and the first bank card was introduced in 1946. During the beginning of the 21st-Century mobile and internet banking came into action and now contactless payment card is commonly used.

Each one of us contributes in our own way to society to earn a living. We use our skills to earn money so that we can purchase all the things we need to live healthy, comfortable and enjoyable lives.

No matter how much money we earn or have, it's our attitude and the value we place upon it that is the most important factor. A person can earn a lot of money and can still have an attitude that they are in lack whereas a person who earns and has very little money has great value for how they attained it and how it enhances their life.

We can become quite complacent about money when we go to work and have money transferred straight into our bank account each week or month. We can end up spending it with equal complacency. Our value for the money we earn or for anything else for that matter can diminish with repetitive experiences.

Increasing our gratitude for money helps to increase our value and respect for how it helps us, how even a very small amount of money can go a long way. We can be grateful also for the work we have done to earn money, placing value on our skills and hard work and understanding how the time and effort we have put into something has been converted to money which we can use to pay for the things we need to support ourselves and our family.

50 percent of the world's workers live with their families on less than $2.50 per person per day and 80 percent of people live on less than $10 per day. This is the stark reality of the world we live in today. It wakes us up to appreciate and respect the money we have no matter how much it may be and increases the value of it greatly.

⚮ Whatever you may be doing to earn a living, value how you are contributing to society in some way. When you spend the money you have earned from your skills, time and effort, feel grateful for the work you did to be able to buy what you need to support yourself and your family, this practice helps to increase the value for yourself, your job, the money and for what you are paying for.

◊ If there is something that you really want to own or experience, which requires money to attain it, but you don't have enough for it yet, then saving bit by bit over time is one of the best ways to increase your gratitude and value of money. Get a plan together of how much you need to put aside each day, week or month to be able to have enough to attain what you want.

✺ A fun way to increase your value and gratitude for money is to use a skill or hobby you have to raise money. It can be providing a service or making things. You can do this on your own or get together a group of people. You can raise money for something you want or for a charity or good cause. Being sponsored by many people to do something for charity is a great way to increase the value for what money can do to help others.

⚮ Look around you now, what has the exchange of money allowed you to have and experience. Generating a greater respect for money, allows us to become more mindful of how we've attained it and how we spend it and how it enhances our life.

⚮ Think back to a time when you had to save for something you wanted. You did something to work towards gaining enough to fulfil a dream or buy something special. Value and reappreciate the whole experience again.

Freedom

"For to be free is not merely to cast off one's chains, but to live in a way that respects and enhances the freedom of others." Nelson Mandela

What is freedom? Let us think about the millions of people throughout history who have not known freedom or who have had it taken away from them and the millions of people who live without freedom at this present moment in our own time. There are people who live in fear and insecurity, fearing for their lives and safety during a war and for the lives and safety of their loved ones; some maybe slaves bought and sold. There are people who are hungry, starved or diseased, living in refugee camps, suffering under torture or immediate threat of death. There are prisoners, people living in concentration camps or death camps. There are children who are made to perform forced labour. Some people are denied even the most basic rights because of their race, religion or nationality.

We take for granted the freedom that we have. Throughout our day we live in freedom and we go through our day-to-day life without realising the freedom that we have. We are free to go where we want, to eat what we wish, to speak from our hearts and minds, to walk where we want to, free to express our thoughts and opinions and our creativity and we have the freedom of choice.

Try to imagine your life without freedom, imagine living is a place where you were confined to an area and were not permitted to leave this area for fear of your safety and life. Imagine living during a war, fearing for your life and not being allowed to express what you think is wrong. Imagine being forced to work or not having enough to feed yourself or your family. It is all hard to imagine, we cannot really know unless we have experienced this lack of freedom but we can express our compassion for all of those who lack freedom and find a way to help them in some way and we can respect and feel grateful for the freedom that we do possess.

♡ Learn from those who have fought for freedom and people who have lived with a lack of freedom. Watch documentaries, speak to, listen to their stories and experiences, read books and research on the internet what people have endured and experienced from a lack of freedom. Many people throughout history and today have fought for their freedom and the freedom of others. We live in a world where so many people do not have the freedom we do, so many of us go about our lives without realising this and we take our freedom for granted. Either from our own experiences or by learning from other people's experiences find ways to raise more awareness and help fight for the freedom of others.

⚕ Many people are trapped in a prison of their own minds or due to circumstances. Many people live in a society or culture or personal situation or in relationships which do not allow the freedom to change. People can feel trapped for many different reasons. It can take great courage to break free from the prisons in our lives, many of which have been self-created. If you feel you lack the freedom you really need or want, look deeply at what it is that is preventing you from having this freedom. Is it your own mind, your situation or circumstance, a person, people around you, your environment, your perceptions, your fear? Find the root cause, direct your love and compassion towards yourself and find the courage within yourself to try and change it, to break free.

⚕ If you feel you lack some kind of freedom in your life, in a particular area of your life, become mindful of your day-to-day living. Change your outlook. Take one aspect of it and think about the freedom you have within it. How would you feel if this freedom was taken away from you?

⚕ If you feel unable to practically escape your own personal prison, or choose not to, where does your prison take you where you feel a sense of freedom, how can you make this place bigger? Feel grateful for this safe feeling.

♡ Remind others around you of the freedom they have especially when they are engaged in negative conversations about what they lack, reminding yourself in the process.

The Wonder of the Body

The body is truly a wonder. From the moment we were conceived, the embryo has all the intelligent information it needs to build the body and all its internal organs. Throughout our lives the body and internal organs know exactly what to do, each part of the body has its specific function to keep us alive. We can appreciate the miracle of the body by placing our awareness on a particular part of the body or internal organ, looking deeply at what it does for us and how it helps us and then feeling grateful for it, sending this part of the body our love and appreciation.

☺ Become aware of the miracle of your body and mind. Ask yourself - What is making my heart beat continuously every second? What allows me to breathe in 7 to 8 litres of air per minute? What created the 100 billion neurons in my brain? How does the digestive system, and all the other parts of the body know exactly what to do to keep me functioning well? We can only be in absolute awe and gratitude for the miracle of the body. The whole body with its entirely different parts works like an orchestra with its different instruments, they perform beautifully together to form an incredible work of art.

☺ Place your awareness on different parts of your body and feel the gratitude for them, send them a heartfelt thank you. Choose one part of the body or internal organ; visualise the body part or find a picture of the body part or organ to meditate on. Look deeply and meditate on all the ways this part of the body or organ helps you. For example the heart; the heart is an incredible organ. It allows blood and oxygen to flow to every part of your body and helps to carry the waste products of your cells to the areas where they can be dealt with. Your lungs allow you to take in fresh oxygen and send it to all your cells giving them energy and life and also helps eliminate waste carbon dioxide into the atmosphere. Your stomach and intestines are breaking down all the food that you eat into smaller pieces so that they can be passed into the bloodstream and into all the cells of your body to provide them with nutrients. You could do some research on different parts of the body to understand their function more deeply, every part of your body is silently, behind the scenes doing an incredible service for you.

☺ There are about 50 trillion cells in the body all carrying out their different functions. In meditation take a journey inside your body, into your cells. Many of our cells have different life spans, they carry out their functions then they die to be born again into new cells. Feel grateful for all your cells, trillions of cells working together as one unit to give you the gift of life.

☺ Give thanks to your body while washing it, putting clothes on it. Nurture it by giving parts of your body a nice massage; you may want to use some oil, absorbing with each stroke your grateful loving kindness.

☺ Give your internal organs a good massage. Your diaphragm is a muscle that separates the abdominal organs from your lungs and heart. As you take an in-breathe the diaphragm expands as the lungs and ribs expand pushing down upon the abdominal organs – the stomach, liver, intestines, reproductive organs. As you breathe out fully the diaphragm contracts pushing up on the lungs and heart, massaging these organs. As you do some deep breathing, visualise and feel your diaphragm moving and flowing up and down massaging your internal organs.

☺ Engage in activities which celebrate and allow you to become greatly aware of your body. Activities such as a sport, yoga, tai-chi, qigong, martial arts, dancing, singing, arts, and crafts, playing a musical instrument. Learn a new skill that engages the body. Celebrate the amazing things your body can do. Notice how you gradually refine the body with a new skill, where eventually the body knows innately exactly what to do and how. The mind and body working in tune together.

☺ Body Scan Meditation - Sitting comfortably on a chair or lying down close your eyes and send your awareness to different parts of your body. Starting from your feet work your way up the body; focusing on relaxing. As you breathe, send your feelings of gratitude into each part. You could imagine light flowing up the body as you travel with your mind to each part. This light has loving, healing energies and can be any colour you like. You could visualise the energy flowing up your body as anything that fills you with love. Be creative in what you wish to flow through your body during this meditation. As you travel to each part, breathe into it.

The Amazing Duo

Our arms, hands, and fingers are truly amazing. If we really think about all the things our arms and hands do for us the list would be very long.

☺ Watch your hands and fingers movements whilst doing something. Watch carefully how they perform intricate fine motion tasks. Notice the strength and versatility they require to allow you to do a huge variety of tasks.

☺ Sense of touch – close your eyes and ask someone to place an object in your hands. Use your hands and fingers to sense the object, see how long it takes for you to recognise what it is.

☺ Many of the actions we perform require both arms and hands, but we are naturally either right-handed or left-handed. We use one arm and hand more than the other, very few of us are ambidextrous, able to use both hands equally well. Try to engage in some kind of activity that uses the other hand, always working together with its partner, but allowing the lesser-used arm and hand to start building the muscles and memory and abilities to help more. You'll start to become much more mindful of your arms and hands by this exercise, developing a greater appreciation for how much they allow you to do. Try brushing your teeth with your other hand, washing up, eating, cleaning, picking something up, placing it somewhere, opening the door, using the pc mouse, try writing with your non-dominant hand. You could also try drawing or painting with your other hand. Whatever it looks like it will be something that wasn't easy to achieve but is special. You can make a very special gift for someone, something created by your non-dominant hand. You'll start using the part of your brain that trains the side of your body to do these actions more naturally. Using the other hand more opens up creativity, improves intelligence, balances our brain function; allow both parts of our arms and hands to work together much more efficiently. At first, it will be quite awkward and interesting to see what happens and also quite amusing as you try these exercises, it will greatly increase your gratefulness for your wonderful arms and hands.

A Journey of Thousand Miles

Our legs and feet are incredible. Each step we take carries us to wherever we want to go. They carry the weight of our whole body. All the muscles, nerves, joints and bones in our legs and feet move us forward in the direction our mind wants us to go.

The average person's stride length is approximately 2.5 feet long. That means it takes just over 2,000 steps to walk one mile, therefore most of us on average walk a few thousand steps a day just going about our day-to-day activities, so we have a lot to be grateful for to our legs and feet as they work exceptionally hard for us. Taking steps with our legs and feet helps to improve our general health. With each step, our heart pumps blood around our body which helps transport nutrients to all parts of our body. They increase the oxygen into our lungs and into our brain and into all our cells. They help to move our whole bodies so we can exercise and strengthen all our muscles, joints and bones. Knowing and understanding this, we can become more mindful and appreciative of each step taken with our legs and feet.

☺ When you are walking, try to become more mindful of your legs and feet, notice how they move. Start with your feet and toes, notice the heel touches the ground first, then the soles of the foot, then the toes. Notice how while one foot is on the ground the other is lifted off the ground, the weight of your whole body is temporarily on one foot and on your toes. Your ankles which attach your lower legs to your feet, help you move your body forward, your knee joints also help propel your body forward as well as your joints in the upper part your legs. Just imagine if you did not have these flexible joints in your legs, you would find it very difficult to walk. Now think of all the muscles and tendons in your legs, the strength in them must be enormous; to carry the weight of your body considering that on average we walk a few thousand steps each day. With each step, send your legs and feet your gratitude. Send warm loving grateful energy to them when they are resting. Give them a grateful massage to show your care for them.

A Walk of Gratitude

"Take my hand, we will walk, we will only walk, we will enjoy our walk without thinking of arriving anywhere." Thich Nhat Hanh

☺ Go on a mindful walk. There are so many things that we can become aware of and feel grateful for while we are walking. There may be other people around you while you are walking, so you can feel grateful for their presence around you. There may be nature around you, so you could feel gratitude for being around the beautiful energy of nature. Walking in nature is like a nutritious drink for the soul. There may be houses of many kinds around you, so you could feel grateful that they give shelter and a home to so many people. Take pleasure in looking at people's front garden as you walk by them. There may be shops that you pass on your walk, you could look at some of the items in the shop windows and find something that you see to feel gratitude for. As you walk along, notice and really look at what is around you, see things from a different frame of mind. By being mindful and aware of what is around you while walking, you enhance your experience and create a wonderful walk of gratitude. Everything around you becomes more alive and gains value when it is touched by your awareness and gratitude.

☺ If you walk a familiar route to somewhere regularly, change the route. Step away from what you are used to and walk another path. Changing familiar patterns opens up a whole new world.

☺ While you are walking, either on our own or with other people, on your way to somewhere or walking for pleasure, open up your awareness and look all around you. Gradually allow your awareness to expand to your surroundings. Take in the sights, sounds, and smells of each thing that captures your attention. Consider the feelings and emotions these things provoke. Look at the path you are walking on, look at the sky, what do you see around you? Scan the whole area around you. Focus your attention on specific things. Notice the shapes, textures, contours. What colours can you see? What can you smell? What can you hear? These sounds could be close by or far off in the distance.

Stop occasionally on your walk and look around you, when you see something that catches your eyes, observe it for a while. What do you feel? When you have given it your full awareness and gratitude you can walk on and stop again along the way. Choose one thing on your walk that you have noticed and give it more of your attention, think of all the ways that you can be grateful for it. You may find that when you have felt gratitude for one thing on your walk, you will start to see many other things to feel gratitude for. Your awareness becomes sharper and you become more mindful and present.

☺ On your walk, take a moment to stop and close your eyes, closing your visual sense. Open up your hearing sense and listen carefully, pick up the sounds. What can you hear? This can open up a whole new realm of sound. Whatever it may be, enjoy the experience and feel the gratitude. After a while open your eyes again and take in the full tapestry of colour and light before you, how much more vibrant do the colours look, do you notice anything different that you hadn't noticed before?

☺ Simply enjoy your walk, becoming mindful of your steps. Focus on the physical sensation of walking. Notice the lifting and falling of your foot, the movements in your legs and body. Become aware of your feet as they touch the ground, the motion of your legs, arms, hips and back as you walk. Become grateful for the parts of your body that allows you to walk. Engage your whole body in the experience. Focus on a particular part of your body and notice its movements, notice what other parts of your body it's connected to. Become aware of the sensations you feel, the wind on your cheeks, the texture of clothing on your skin. Become aware of how your whole body flows wonderfully. Walking can be a beautiful dance-like act, it has its own rhythm and pace, it's physical but also connected to the mind; it's yogic in nature. Every time you walk, enjoy the dance with the ground and your surroundings. Make every walk a walk of gratitude, wherever you are.

⚖ Remember fondly some of your favourite walks. Feel grateful for some of the places where you have experienced a lovely walk. Visualise some the aspects of the walk you remember. In meditation visualise a walk somewhere new. Engage your senses in the experiences.

One Hundred Gifts

"When you arise in the morning, think of what a privilege it is to be alive, to breathe, to think, to enjoy, to love." Marcus Aurelius

The practice of 100 gifts can be done in written form, on paper or electronically, speech recorded, as a blog, photo book, image scrapbook, sketchbook, video clips, collection of symbols or a mix of all.

�butterfly Set yourself a challenge of 100 things you are grateful for without repeating yourself, seek and find treasure in everything. Include -

- Your relationships - family, friends, teachers
- Achievements
- Personal qualities and character traits
- Assets (things you own or things given to you)
- Memorable experiences (places you've visited and things you've done)
- Other challenges (which you have overcome or learned from)
- Health (good health and health challenges that you have overcome and learned from)
- Things from nature
- Parts of the body
- Positive habits created, perceptions changed
- The thoughtful actions of other people
- Include things from the past, present, and future

✿ If it helps you could divide your list into different categories or even create your 100 gifts for each different category.

♡ Get family, friends, and children involved to create their own one hundred gifts project, then share with each other your lists or creations.

✿ Focus your 100 gifts on the future or everything that you would like to create in your life. Use the categories above to help you. Your energy of gratefulness in the present will project itself into the future, you are planting seeds in your heart and mind to achieve these things opening up and creating all the possibilities for the future.

Timelessness of Gratitude

Gratitude is timeless. We can be grateful for so much that has passed; so much in the present moment and so much of what is yet to come. By being grateful for things of the past you become more aware of the resources and lessons that will help you move forward into the future. Being grateful for things in the future opens your mind to the possibilities of making things happen. Let us travel through 20 years of gratitude; the past, present, and future. This practice can be done by yourself or with someone else, in meditation or written down.

👁 In the first part of this exercise, we travel back in time. Think of something you are grateful for now from a month ago. It could be something that you didn't feel grateful for at the time, but in hindsight, you are now thankful. Now do the same exercise for something within 1 year ago, then within 5 years ago and then again within 10 years ago. It could be a person you knew or an event or experience, anything that brings back the feelings of gratitude. Travel back in time, picking out those moments that were special to you or that changed your life or perspective.

👁 Now think of something that you are grateful for at this present moment or something that you'd like to do right now.

👁 In the last part of this practice we are travelling forward in time to the future. Think of something that you would like to do or experience in a month's time, something you know you will be grateful for; even the feelings of anticipation of what you'd like to do is generating thankfulness in this present moment. By bringing this intention into your consciousness you have already set a foundation to make it happen and that's an exciting and grateful thought. Now do the same for something you'd like to do, experience or change within 1 year's time into the future, then within 5 years from now and finally within 10 years time from now.

These are suggested time periods but you can adopt your own timescales for this practice.

Missing You

"Everything is a gift. The degree to which we are awake to this truth is a measure of our gratefulness, and gratefulness is a measure of our aliveness." Brother David Steindl-Rast

One way of helping to increase our gratitude for the people in our life and the things around us and our experiences is to imagine not having them in our life anymore. Oftentimes we take for granted what we do have, we are not mindful of them. We get so used to the things and people around us that we eventually stop appreciating them, we even complain about them, and we sometimes think we deserve something better than we already have. We then only start to appreciate them when they are not there anymore, or if something is coming to an end, or if they have been taken away from us.

If these feelings of missing them when they are not there generate feelings of gratitude, why not imagine you miss them now so that you create the feelings of appreciation for what you already have in this present moment.

👁 Think of something that you have in your life at this present moment that gives you great comfort, such as your home or a particular room in your home, or a particular item in your home, appliances, electricity, heating, water, shower and so on. It could be your car, the fuel that runs your car, your job. It can be your ability to see and hear, your ability to walk, your health. Choose one thing now. Imagine losing it, imagine your life without it, what would your life be like, how would it alter your life, how would you cope without it? Can you remember a time when you did not have this thing in your life, even if it was for a short time? What did it feel like? How did it feel getting it back again into your life?

👁 Imagine something you love in your life coming to an end; a relationship, a job, an experience, you are moving home. Knowing that it will soon be coming to an end, how grateful are you feeling right now about it?

♡ Think about all the people in your life, close family members, friends, work colleagues, your community. Oftentimes we can get irritated with those around us, but imagine your life without them. In so many ways we are helped, supported and comforted by the people in our lives. From the people who are part of your life, choose a particular person; now imagine they are not in your life anymore, how would you feel, how would your life change? Feelings of gratitude will arise for this person; you will start to see them in a different light, your attitude towards them will change, the energy of being around them will turn into something more positive and they will feel your appreciation and value for them.

◉ How would your life have been without a particular experience, an achievement, an opportunity given? What about all the special moments you have had with your family, friends, and community, all the many different kinds of teachers in your life? Think of some beneficial experiences and opportunities that have helped you grow and learn and that have led you to many other opportunities and experiences. Choose one experience now, take it out of your life; notice what feelings arise in you? Imagine you had never had this experience, how would your life be now without it. Take it away altogether and your feelings of gratitude and appreciation for that experience is bound to increase, even if they were exceptionally challenging at the time.

⚖ Try going some time without something – your car, books, internet, water, gas, electricity, a shower, your mobile, food – how did you manage without them? How much did you miss them? Become mindful of the feelings that arise throughout your day. Turn these feelings of missing them into appreciation and value.

♡ Express your feelings of appreciation for someone by telling them how much you miss them when they are not around. Choose something specific about them that you miss.

♡ Choose something about yourself that you would miss if you didn't have it. A quality, a positive habit, a personality trait. What kind of person would you be without it? How would it change your life? Who or what would be affected by it? Appreciate your specialness.

My Aspirations for Gratitude

"Hope is the thing with feathers that perches in the soul – and sings the tunes without the words – and never stops at all." Emily Dickinson

⚘ What do you aspire to be grateful for? What are the hopes within yourself for cultivating gratitude? Here are some questions which will allow you to delve deeper into your mind and feelings to discover your aspirations for gratitude.

- What in my life do I really want to feel grateful for?
- What am I avoiding?
- Who or what makes me feel sad or disappointed rather than happy?
- What habit, perception, attitude or disposition do I wish to change?
- What great quality do I want to cultivate and express in my life?
- What action do I regret from the past?
- Who and what am I finding difficulty liking and in feeling grateful for?
- Who in my life am I taking for granted?
- What makes my life so much easier?
- What am I unhappy about in this present moment?
- What circumstances do I find myself in that I would like to change?
- What future event in my life that I wish for can I feel grateful for right now?

It takes time, patience, understanding, great will, determination, and perseverance to achieve anything you want in life or change something that does not serve you. Make gratitude your aspiration and create a healthier attitude to life.

♡ Pair up with someone and ask each other one of the questions above or choose your own question. It helps to openly share your aspiration for gratitude with someone. Concentrate on one question and see where it leads you. Finding an accountability partner helps you stick to your goal and aspiration. Checking in with someone else on your progress helps you stay committed to your gratitude practice. You'll make greater positive changes sharing your practice with someone else.

Calendar Moments

Calendars remind us of those special events during the year; national holidays, birthdays, events, things to do, appointments, anniversaries. We can use a calendar in a creative way to plan our practices of gratitude. Buy a calendar or use one on your pc or mobile or make your own calendar.

� On your calendar set up a schedule of different gratitude practices for each day or week, emphasising a different focus for each day, or week. You could use some of the practices in this book. To make it more random you could number the day or week with a page number from this book and when you come to the day or week look up the page and read it and practice one or more of the practices written on the page or make your own up about the subject you have read about.

✿ Use special events, holidays, birthdays, appointments as prompts to practice gratitude relating to the day. Use birthdays to appreciate a person and their qualities or use holidays as appreciating travel and everything relating to travel or having a break. Whatever appointment you have, become more mindful during the day and make it an opportunity to practice gratitude within it.

◊ Look up and make a note of special spiritual days or national holidays within the various traditions or international days observed by the United Nations. So many of these special days practice a form of gratitude, so it would be lovely to join in with the celebrations.

✎ On each day of your calendar write down something that happened during the day that you are grateful for: a happy moment, a wonderful awareness, an inspiring moment, a great insight, a change in perception; something that lifted your spirits. Keep it short and sweet, writing down one word or one sentence on each day.

✿ Create a photo calendar; paper or digital version. One photo for each day of the year representing something you are grateful for.

Step Back in Time

Ah, the good old days! is often what we find ourselves saying from time to time when we are reminded of the past. We smile and think back to a period of time in the past in which we believe life to have been simpler and better.

In every era of our lives, we face challenges, yet as time passes many of us look back fondly and remember the good points, and we alter in our minds our experiences and feelings of the past (however joyful or challenging they were) into something we can learn from.

With the ever-increasing times of change, where technology is advancing rapidly and the population of the Earth is accelerating, there seems to be more consumption, more consumerism, more waste, more pollution, too many TV channels and somehow less time as people work more and more or are travelling in a car and have very little time left for themselves, their families or friends. We smile at the past, perhaps as far back as our childhood when things were simpler. We may have owned less or consumed less, but we were content with what we had. The things we used lasted longer, were of a better quality, and we used them to its maximum capability and recycled and reused when we could. There was a greater appreciation for the people and things around us, it was all enough to live and be happy with.

👁 Let us step back in time. If you had a time machine, when and where in the past would you go? Who would you meet and want to thank in the past? It could be someone from your past that you knew; it could be an inventor of something that you love to use or makes a difference in your life. It could be a teacher from your past who said or did something which positively affected your life. Meet them in your past and thank them wholeheartedly.

🦋 Have a 'no car day'. Choose a day where you don't use the car and try and find things to do during the day which don't require getting in a car and driving somewhere.

�butterfly Have a no-technology for entertainment day once a week, this means no TV, computers, tablets, mobiles, radios, etc. Play board games or cards. Have a nice meal together as a family rather than watching TV while eating. Go for a walk together with a friend or family member or on your own. Read a book or read to each other, sing songs together, paint, cook together or share stories. Write a letter to someone instead of sending an email or text message. People in the past found many ways to enjoy their time together without technology, we can do the same. Appreciate all those moments without technology.

🍎 Try and grow some of your own herbs and vegetables. You can start small by using a pot and growing your own herbs, or a bigger pot to grow vegetables. Research what you need and try it out. It's a great feeling to grow your own food, nurturing it as it grows and savouring the taste of it in your meals. Next time you go to the grocery store, you'll have a greater appreciation for the food you see and understand a little more of the time and care it takes to grow them.

♡ Unlike the mass production of many things these days, things of the past took time, effort, discipline to make. Use and appreciate something from the past – an old tool, furniture, a book, clothing, something that has stood the test of time and still has a use and value to this day.

👁 Think of a time in your life which brings back feelings of fondness or nostalgia. In meditation ignite these fond feelings into your mind. Allow the memory of the experience to fill your heart again. Smiling at the memory, whisper a thank you to it. Feeling grateful for having this experience in the past and now again in the present moment. Every time we recall a memory from the past we alter it in some way depending on our present state of consciousness. With a mindset of gratitude our feelings relating to the memory are always enhanced. Try and re-live in your mind and heart happy moments from your past every day. Recapture images and feelings during the experience.

♡ Share with someone a happy memory from the past. Try to remember it with as much detail as possible. How did you feel then and how do you feel now talking about it?

No Mud, No Lotus

"Most people are afraid of suffering. But suffering is a kind of mud to help the lotus flower of happiness grow. There can be no lotus flower without the mud." Thich Nhat Hanh

Thich Nhat Hanh's words speak great truth. We can feel happiness more deeply, we can appreciate the happy moments more deeply if we have experienced pain and suffering. We may not always see the lotus while we are in the mud, but it is always there ready to bloom when the time is right.

We can all think back to a time in our past which was very difficult and challenging, whether it was to do with our health, our relationships, our work, a traumatic experience, a time in which we suffered emotionally, mentally or physically. Life will always set us challenges from time to time, some small, some life-changing, they may have seemed very difficult at the time, but we will always get through them, with the help of others or our own innate strength and wisdom.

Think of all the times in which you did get through a difficult, challenging experience. Think of all you learned during this time, how your perspective changed, about yourself, the situation and life in general. You may be going through a difficult time in this present moment, and perhaps you cannot see the lotus or the light at the end of the tunnel but they are there right at its heart of your suffering. If you can be grateful for the growth in your spirit within the experience, the relationship, the situation that is making you suffer right at this moment, then you will find your pain easing. During times of adversity ask yourself – Is there something about this situation I can learn from, benefit from, that I can be grateful for?

If you can see what is around you and within you to be grateful for, in spite of the pain and suffering, then you have found a way to help yourself and those around you and there lies the seed of a wise and beautiful lotus. A lotus which will ultimately bloom to lift your heart and the hearts of others. See pain and suffering as the fertile compost nourishing the seeds of gratitude to grow into beautiful flowers. When time passes you can look back at what you have learned, how you have grown, how you have changed for the better from the experience.

✎ Think of an experience in your life that was challenging, in which you suffered a great deal. On a piece of paper write the challenge on the top. Underneath this make a list of the emotions you felt during this time, the many challenges within the challenge, the new people you met during this time, what did you do to help yourself through this challenge? Who are the people you turned to during this time? Anything you can remember that you experienced during this time. Now make another list underneath of all the ways in which you changed, what you learned, what experiences you've had since, the people you've met since, where it has taken your life. How did this experience change the path of your life? What happy, fulfilling, heartopening experiences have you had since, experiences in which now you feel extremely grateful for? If you don't wish to write then this practice can be done as a meditation or talked through with a trusted friend or family member. Share a story about an experience that at first seemed unpleasant, negative, or even traumatic, which in time you came to understand deeply as a time of great change and growth.

♡ If you are experiencing pain at this moment, think of ways you can help yourself; practice gratitude, search out people or groups who can help you, search within yourself for the wisdom and strength you already hold from past experiences to help you through. Nurture the seeds of gratitude. Every difficulty carries within it the seeds of an equal or greater benefit. There is a Buddhist teaching called Impermanence. Everything is impermanent, that includes both suffering and happiness, nothing lasts forever neither happiness or pain. All we can do is learn from the pain and be grateful for the moments of happiness that are all around us if we can open our minds, hearts, and eyes to see them.

⚬ Think of someone that you know that's turned their mud into a lotus. Look at a historical figure or someone in the public eye or someone you know who has transformed a personal challenge into something beautiful. Be inspired by their life story.

The Memory of Written Words

"Fill your paper with breathings of your heart." William Wordsworth

The written word has a memory. When we write down our thoughts, feelings, and experiences we create an imprinted hard copy of them and can read them again at any time in the future. Keeping a gratitude journal is a very good way of noting down what you are grateful for. In a day of routine, we can forget to stop and appreciate moments that are special, however small and fleeting they may be. Usually, a thought comes to us and then just as quickly as the thought came in it goes away and is replaced by another thought. Remembering to write our thoughts and feelings and experiences down whether we write them on paper or type our words electronically is a wonderful way to preserve our gratefulness and memory. We can read and look back and almost relive our gratitude in our hearts all over again and learn from the wisdom of our own words.

✎ Create your own gratitude journal. Start by writing one gratitude a day, either on paper or electronically, it could be one sentence long or a few sentences or a page, it all depends on how much you enjoy writing and how much time you have. You could write in your journal during the day or at the end of the day. Choose one thing during your day to be grateful for. It could be anything where you stopped and noticed, something that you saw, you felt, you learned, you heard, you did, something someone else did, a momentary grateful thought or a deep gratitude. On a normal day, you would have barely noticed it. By looking back at your day and writing down your thoughts, feelings, and experiences of gratitude you will increase its value, and your joy and appreciation of that moment are captured and continued beautifully within the memory of your written words. You can write about your experiences on anything that comes into your mind and heart, something you cherish and can be reminded of in the future when you read it again from your journal.

♡ Encourage someone you know to start their own gratitude journal.

✏ You can make your journal specific, concentrating on a particular subject each week. Here are some examples:

- Look out for those things that give you great comfort
- The people you are grateful for; the kind things they have done for you or for other's; their qualities, how they've inspired you
- Different aspects of nature
- Unexpected surprises
- Changes in your attitude and perceptions
- Different parts of your body
- Things that didn't go well but you can find something to be grateful for within them
- Your wonderful qualities
- Moments of joy and laughter
- Gratitude relating to food, nutrition, health and wellness

Choose a different subject each week. Be creative. There are many ideas from this book that you can use. Set a challenge of not repeating the same gratitude – write down something different on each day.

✏ Look ahead and write down something each day that you would like to manifest into your life; a goal, a dream, a change in attitude, a new relationship, making a difference, more confidence to do something you've always wanted to do, travel somewhere. Write down how grateful you are now for it even though it's not happened yet, feel how wonderful it is. Generate positive, elevated emotions and feel the gratitude for it now in this present moment as if it has already happened.

✏ Write a gratitude journal for someone you care about; someone with whom you have shared many moments with. Each day write down something about this person for which you are grateful. Include happy experiences shared, wonderful qualities you admire about them, things you have learned from them, things they have done for you and how they've helped you. When completed, give it to them as your grateful gift.

✏ Write a poem or a song to express the gratitude you feel for something or someone. Share it with others so they too can be inspired.

Time Traveller

"Give thanks for unknown blessings already on their way." Native American Saying

Our life spans many years into the past, is this very moment in the present and also contains all that is to come well into the future. In reality, we are timeless. We are made up of many factors, conditions, ancestors that date back to infinity. All of these factors in our past have brought us to this present moment. The present moment is made of everything that has passed and is also made up of everything that is yet to come well into the future, to infinity. Everything we experience and are grateful for now draws a map into our future. If our attitude and approach to life are grateful, it will carry through to the rest of our future and also attract more experiences of gratitude into our lives.

⚶ Not only can we change our perception of the past in the present moment, we can change our perception of the future in the present moment. Project your gratitude into the future, give thanks for the experiences you will have. They may be unknown to you but look forward to them, get excited about your future. Know for sure that your future will be filled with many joyful, inspiring, funny, heartfelt, surprising, touching moments that you are sure to be grateful for. Be grateful for them in this present moment.

◉ Look back into your past and think of something that you always wanted to experience and how you made it happen. How grateful you felt when it happened; a dream came true, an aspiration fulfilled. Think of something now that you wish to experience in the future or wish to achieve. Visualise it happening, hold it in your heart, how does it feel? How grateful do you feel? Visualise your future wish as much as possible throughout your day and in meditation. Visualise it in as much detail as possible and be grateful for every moment of the journey.

♡ Share some of your time-travelling experiences with someone. Talk about something you are grateful for in the past, and what you looking forward to in the future.

⚘ If you have a certain perception of a past event that is negative, look forward to changing it in the future to something healthier. Generate the thoughts and feelings right now of how you would like to feel about it in your future. Decide how it will change your life for the better and visualise it happening.

⚘ So many of us become despondent about the human race. We seem to focus on the negative. Let us be more optimistic about the future of the human species on this Planet. There has been a lot of destruction along the way of human civilisation, but there has also been a lot of learning, change, and progress in looking after our Planet and each other. Human consciousness is expanding at a rapid rate, so we should be grateful for the great leaps of mankind in creating a more harmonious world. Look back at the many wonderful things that people have achieved to help the Planet; how we've invented the many environmentally friendly ways to provide fuel. How we've created ways to recycle, how we're planting trees; how different communities come together to support one another; how we care and protect other species we share the Planet with; what about the countless ways we provide healthcare to so many. There are so many ways in which humans are trying to protect our environment and help each other. Become more mindful of the many wonderful aspects of humans and what they are doing to help, learn and change. Look at how you personally are helping to create a more harmonious world. By practising gratitude you are helping enormously. Next time you find yourself complaining about something, ask yourself "What can I do to help the situation?" Find more ways in which you can get involved and feel grateful that you are doing your bit for the world.

⚘ Look to the future of the human species. Let us look upon it with hope. Judging from how people have always found a way to try and make things better and learn from the past, we can be grateful for what we will be able to do going forward. Grateful for the growing consciousness, excited about what we will learn and all the generations who will find ways to live more harmoniously with each other and the environment. Be grateful for all the wonderful new inventions that humans will come up with and for all the incredible new discoveries. It's an exciting future and it's far better to be hopeful and contribute in our own way to make it better for ourselves and for future generations.

Ageless Spirit

"The best thing in life is to go ahead with all your plans and your dreams, to embrace life and to live every day with passion, to lose and still keep the faith and to win while being grateful. All of this because the world belongs to those who dare to go after what they want. And because life is really too short to be insignificant." Charlie Chaplin

Age is more about our attitude than the number of years we have lived. We need to be grateful for whatever age we are, just to be alive is a miracle and a great gift. Everyone's life is unique. It's a personal journey, filled with joys and sadness, love and inspiration, accomplishments and learning. Our life makes up a beautiful colourful tapestry. We cannot see the darker shades without the lighter shades and we cannot see the lighter shades without the darker shades, together all shades of colours make up the portrait of our life. As soon as we are born our life has a story to tell. As we get older we experience more, we learn more and steer our life in many directions, and with each decision we make we write our life story. With every thought we think we are creating our life.

Every year we celebrate our birthdays, we celebrate our life with those we love. No matter how old we are, it is always a celebration to be alive. We are all spirit, not a number. We are love, joy, happiness, laughter, students, teachers, wisdom, compassion, and much more. We are made up of all the beautiful values and qualities that go beyond the number of years we have lived and this is absolutely something to celebrate and be grateful for.

Feel grateful for whatever age you are. It's what we make of the years we have in our life that is important. See yourself as a being of love and light, with wonderful qualities and special gifts that will continue on well past the number of your age. Feel grateful to be a human; that you have the ability to love, to change your perceptions and have the consciousness to be mindful and appreciate everything around you.

♡ Children are so innocent and say and see things as they are. They possess an exuberant imagination and live entirely in the present moment. They see the world around them with fresh new eyes, they are constantly learning and absorbing new things and their curiosity is boundless. Change the lens of your adult's eyes to the lens of a child's eyes, what do you see? Be grateful for the child that is always there within you. Talk to a child and ask them questions on how they see the world around them. The true honesty of children can make us smile. What they say can teach us so much. They notice things that we wouldn't normally see and they describe it in the loveliest, funniest way. Allow them to magically ignite the playful curiosity of the child within you. In some way, we are all young at heart. We all have the spirit of a child; fun, laughter, wonder, and joy for life. Find ways to be more young at heart. Do something that you loved to do as a child, have fun, laugh. Being around children helps to bring out the child in us. They are not afraid to be happy and silly because it's their true nature.

♡ Celebrate the years you have lived on this Planet. Write down or talk to someone about your experiences in life, what you loved, what you learned, what you love about this present moment, what you are looking forward to and what you would love to do in the future. Celebrate your life and make the most of every moment you are given.

⚖ Many people think they are too old to do certain things in their life, to accomplish certain dreams, but we are never too old. Anything can be accomplished at any age; studying for a degree, travelling, changing career, learning a new skill, starting a family, anything at all. It just takes the will and passion to reach for your dreams. Be grateful for all the dreams you have already made real and all the dreams you still can make real. First, look back at all the dreams you had in the past that you actualised, that came true. How did it make you feel, were they even better than you dreamed possible? Did you even care how old you were then; you just went for it and made them happen. Now write down the dreams you have at this moment, start to believe that they are possible and start to put actions in place to make them into reality and remember it is the journey to the destination that is the most important and enriching part.

Visiting Your Past Self

"No man ever steps in the same river twice, for it's not the same river and he's not the same man." Heraclitus

If we had a time machine, there would certainly be times in our lives that we would go back to and relive and experience again, those moments from our past that we treasure; happy, joyous, inspiring, poignant moments. But there are also experiences and moments from our past that we would change if we could, moments that we may regret or that were very unpleasant, a time of pain. We would make different decisions which would have taken our lives in another direction, onto another path. But we don't have a time machine, the only thing that we can do in this present moment is be grateful for all that has passed, all our experiences, good and unpleasant, happy and sad, all our decisions from our past. We cannot change our past, but we can travel back in time with our minds and hearts and be grateful for all that we have learned from our past.

Life is a precious gift and an incredible journey of self-discovery. Whatever has happened in our lives up to now has been a journey to discover ourselves deeply and our connection with everyone and everything around us. All of our past experiences shape our future decisions and actions and have made us who we are today.

Our minds store away our experiences and emotions from our past. We can access them at any time, bringing these memories into our consciousness. We can visit our past self again, travel back in time through our minds and hearts. But every time we make a journey into our past the experience is different each time because our perception of them has changed. It is also very easy to be hard on ourselves, critical of the decisions that we took. The past for us is a fading memory, it's not accurate, and we cannot fully experience the same reality that the person then was facing. The past is fluid according to the state of the present moment. Our interpretation of the past changes, when we go back we visit a different past each time, but if we carry the message of gratitude with us to our past it alters our perception and experience of it every time.

◉ When you have a quiet moment, meditate and think back to a time or a moment in your life that gave you happiness and joy. Visit yourself in that moment and feel gratitude for it. Feel grateful for the experience, the people you were with, the place where you were, the feelings and emotions that you felt. Can you remember any of the small details that meant something special to you?

◉ Think back to a moment when you felt inspired by a person or an event, or a place, or something you've seen or read or listened to, anything that inspired you. Travel back in time in your mind and heart to a time you were inspired and be grateful for it. What made it so inspiring? What did it lead you to do? How did it give you purpose? How did it change the direction of your life?

◉ In meditation travel back in your mind to a difficult time in your life, a time when you experienced pain and suffering, physically or emotionally, or both. Allow your present self to be with your past self in this moment. Your present self would not be here today without the strength you showed during the pain and suffering of your past self. Send back your love to your past self; send back words of comfort, reassuring your past self that it will be ok; you will take this pain and use it to help others, to understand others, to spiritually grow, you will transform the pain into something very beautiful. What would you say to your past self? Can you now see any good that came out of the situation? Can you now send back your gratitude for the experience?

◉ Go back to a time when you had a special experience with a person, visit your past self with this person again. Thank them for their company, their spirit, their joy, and wisdom. Feel grateful for them in that moment again. How did they help you, guide you, how were they there for you, what were their special qualities? Bring this person back into your heart from your past and express your appreciation to them. Bring back a particularly special moment, perhaps a word or a gesture. They may not be here with you now, but they will benefit from the grateful energy you are feeling and expressing towards them wherever they may be.

The Passage of Time

"The world exists as you perceive it. It is not what you see... but how you see it. It is not what you hear... but how you hear it. It is not what you feel... but how you feel it." Rumi

🧘 There are many moments in life where we are made to wait; when our day is brought to a momentary standstill. Standing in the line at the supermarket, watching the kettle boil, waiting for the arrival of a friend, waiting at a traffic light. Whether you're on foot, driving a car, on a bike, or sitting in public transport, it's easy to get slightly annoyed at stop signs. They are slowing you down and preventing you from continuing with your day. Instead of seeing these moments of waiting as a boring inconvenience, treat them as an opportunity to practice some gratitude. Utilise the moments when you are made to wait. Stop, notice your breathing, look around you, what do you see, hear, and feel? Don't reach for the nearest distraction, just be in the moment. Appreciate the mini-breaks life provides you. Use those enforced pauses to your advantage and treat them as little opportunities to exercise mindfulness and gratitude. Every time you have to wait at a stop sign, notice your breathing and look around at where you are and what is going on. See all the other people around you, hear the various noises of the daily bustle, try to be in the moment and enjoy it rather than impatiently waiting for the moment to end. There's a lot you can notice in a few seconds.

"A good traveller has no fixed plans, and is not intent on arriving." Lao Tzu

🧘 While travelling take the opportunity to be mindfully grateful. Focus on the sights and sounds of the passage you are travelling on, the landscapes, the scenery and buildings you pass, other vehicles, the movement of other travellers. Be aware of any feelings and emotions that arise. Don't worry about reaching your destination too quickly, appreciate and savour your travelling experience.

Just Being

"How beautiful it is to do nothing, and then rest afterward."
Spanish Proverb

What is it to be? Being can be described as our true nature, our essence, our spirit, our soul, our inner self. How wonderful it is to be truly ourselves, right here in the present moment, without having to do anything in particular or go anywhere in particular, just being. Really that's the most important part of being human. In this beautiful place of being, the past fades away, the future is too far away to be of any importance, only the wonderful present moment exists.

⚜ Take time to just be. Sit quietly somewhere. Notice how in this state of just being your heart expands and you become acutely aware of life within you and around you. Life in all its beauty becomes clearer and sharper and you become aware of your feelings more deeply. There's no need to rush, strive, achieve, pursue and grasp at life. The qualities of peace, love, joy, and gratitude naturally arise within us when we are truly ourselves in the here and now.

⚜ During your day, stop for a moment and watch the world go by. Let the world speak to you through its very being. While you are with people, become present in your own being and watch the people around you, observe what people are doing. When you are in a busy town or city, watch the world around, become a detached observer, perhaps become mindful of the thoughts that pop into your mind, and then gently direct your awareness back to observing. Sit in nature somewhere and see the beauty it paints for us in every moment. Become aware of your body and how you are sitting right now, notice your chest and abdomen rise and fall gently with each breath.

❋ Take a moment and go outside and pick up something you find in nature. A stick, a leaf, a flower, etc. Study it thoroughly for a few minutes. Notice the colours, the shapes, the patterns, the intricacies. Be with it completely here in this wonderful present moment.

The Beauty of Imperfection

"Imperfection is in some sort essential to all that we know in life."
John Ruskin

So often we notice the imperfections of life, within someone or something, within ourselves or our society. The world is certainly not perfect, but it's within our positive perception of the imperfections where the beauty truly lies. Understanding that imperfections are a part of life, we can stop pursuing the perfect life, the perfect job, the perfect partner, the perfect body, the perfect house. We can find the freedom to live within our imperfections. We believe that happiness is only attained when everything is perfect. When we embrace imperfection, we stop trying to chase for happiness in perfection. We find contentment and happiness and joy even in the midst of imperfection. Happiness is fully available to us regardless of our circumstances and by finding beauty in things as they are.

♡ Imperfections allow us to relate to one another better. No one is perfect; we all have our own quirkiness and unique personalities. Take something about yourself that you perceive as imperfect. Look upon it as something special about yourself. Turn around what you think is different, unusual, odd, missing, stands out, as a beautiful aspect of yourself. How does it enhance who you are? Take the same view of other people around you. Embrace the differences. It allows us to stop pretending to be perfect. It allows us to be true, authentic, vulnerable with ourselves and with others.

♡ Most of the time things don't go completely as we'd like them to. Something goes wrong in an event. Someone said or did something not quite right. You made something and it wasn't exactly how you wanted it to be, perhaps something is missing or out of place. There are endless situations that don't fit into what we expect. It's far better to see the funny side of things, embrace the bit that went wrong, that's not right, that's out of place, that's different. Smile at it and see the beauty of it. You'll remember it, or notice it. Perhaps it wants to be noticed and to stand out. Look upon what's not perfect as actually the most special, most beautiful part of the whole thing.

Hands that Feed

"If you can't feed a hundred people, then feed just one" Mother Teresa

So many meals that we have eaten in our lifetime have been prepared and made by someone else. When we were babies, we were given milk by our mothers. When we were children our parents or carers prepared meals for us to eat, to nourish us and to help us grow. As teenagers and young adults, our parents and carers continued to prepare meals for us. At school perhaps we ate school dinners which were prepared by the school dinner staff. As adults, the person or people we live with may make meals for us. Not forgetting you yourself making meals to feed and nourish yourself and other people.

🍎 Think of a special person in your life who cooks your meals. Feel gratitude for this person. You could tell them how grateful you are or write them a "Thank card" or a "Thank you" letter or give them a gift to show your appreciation, you can even express your gratitude for them in the presence of others about their kindness. It will make them feel so valued. Calculate roughly how many meals this person has made for you.

🍎 When you are in a restaurant eating your meal, look down at the meal on your plate and think of all the people who worked and put time and effort into making this meal for you – the chefs, the staff, the people who delivered the food to the restaurant, the waiters, and managers. While you eat, feel grateful for them all and appreciate the meal. You may have paid for the meal, but it still took a great deal of effort by many people to get the food prepared and placed in front of you.

🍎 Appreciate and value yourself when you make a meal for yourself, someone else, friends or your family. Look at the time, love, thoughtfulness, consideration you have put into feeding others.

🍎 Feed the birds, insects or other wild animals in your environment. Buy bird food, and plant flowers that attract insects that love to feed on their nectar.

An Act of Kindness

"Your acts of kindness are iridescent wings of divine love, which linger and continue to lift others long after the sharing." Rumi

We've all been the recipient of the kindness of others, from family and friends or many times from perfect strangers or from an unknown source. True kindness should be given without wanting anything in return; a selfless act, a sincere concern for the wellbeing of others.

Kindness allows us to express our generosity of spirit, understanding, consideration, compassion and our thoughtfulness for the needs of others. Kindness is infectious; a gesture of kindness from someone inspires us to be more kind to others. Kindness touches our heart, allows us to feel a closer connection with those around us, increasing our faith in human nature.

Because kindness increases our bond with others, our relationships become strengthened which means feelings of cooperation and trust are enhanced. Our survival depends on how strong our bonds are with others, so kindness has several health boosting effects. Kindness releases Oxytocin (the bonding chemical), which helps increase the health of the heart. Kindness is related to many other elevated emotions such as love, compassion, joy, and gratitude. It therefore switches on the healing response of the body setting off a series of health-boosting properties, some of which are boosted immune function, anti-inflammatory effects, anti-aging properties, the release of happy feel-good chemicals, improved digestion, enhanced regeneration and repair in the body. All the processes which can bring about healing, wellbeing, and happiness.

♡ Watch out, witness and observe the kindness of those around you.

♡ Do a kind act that nobody finds out about, where nobody is aware that it was you who did it. This can cultivate the intention of doing good without seeking reward. Feel the inner satisfaction of doing a truly selfless deed.

♡ Be kind to yourself. When you hear that discouraging voice in your head, tell yourself something positive. Make time to listen to yourself. Practice self-care. Do something you love. Try and think of different ways to care for yourself. Something new each day.

♡ *"Thousands of candles can be lit from a single candle, and the life of the candle will not be shortened. Happiness never decreases by being shared".* A wonderful saying by the Buddha which conveys the true benefit of kindness and gratitude. In this way gratitude is passed on from one person to another, to flow in many different directions, into the hearts of many. We can show our gratitude for the kindness given to us by paying it forward. Paying it forward means to respond to a person's kindness to oneself by being kind to someone else. When a person feels the kindness towards themselves, they will feel grateful and want to pass kindness and gratitude onto others, without wanting anything in return, other than feeling good about helping someone. Many people will be surprised with unexpected kindness; they will then naturally feel the need to want to return an act of kindness to others. A kind word or action or a simple "thank you" is one of the simplest ways to warm a person's heart. If someone should ask how they can repay the kindness you have shown them, ask them to pay it forward, do something kind for another. Bring a little joy and comfort into somebody else's life.

♡ Thich Nhat Hanh says, *"The most precious gift we can offer others is our presence. When mindfulness embraces those we love, they will bloom like flowers."* Offer someone your true presence.

♡ Find opportunities to give compliments, spread good news, donate blood. One pint of blood can save up to three lives, be a courteous driver, let people merge in front of you. Let someone in a queue (who only has a few items) go in front of you. Stick inspirational and encouraging sticky notes around your neighbourhood, office, library books, school, and other random places. Offer your seat to someone when there aren't any left. Give words of encouragement to someone about their dreams, no matter how big or small they are. Redirect gifts. Instead of having people give you birthday and holiday gifts, ask them to donate gifts or money to a good cause. Think of creative ways to express kindness.

Speaking Kindly of Others

"Kind words can be short and easy to speak, but their echoes are truly endless." Mother Teresa

A lovely way of expressing our gratitude towards others is to speak kindly of them to others. A common habit that we all possess is talking to others about someone in an unkind way when they are not around, behind their backs, but a lot of the time it's not very pleasant, we gossip about them, we complain about them or we are irritated by them. When we don't like something someone does, we find ourselves being judgemental towards them. Others then join us in speaking and thinking unpleasantly and judgementally about someone else. We do the same with people we don't know personally; we voice our negative opinions about them. Sometimes we join negative judgement conversations that others start. Somehow we get into a habit, but we know it's not very kind of us. We may think that sharing our feelings of negativity about others will help us let go of our feelings but it ultimately makes us feel bad, it makes other's around us feel bad and it doesn't solve anything. When you find yourself thinking negative thoughts toward someone else or something else, could this thought be a generalisation, is it possible that it's not absolutely true, if so then is it just gossip? Perhaps you'd like to delve deeper into yourself and others as to where habits of thinking and speaking about others in unkind ways come from.

A great way to turn this around is to speak more kindly of someone to others. There is always something good to find in everyone, a good quality that they have, something good that they have done or said, a character trait that you admire. Speaking with others about these qualities will help change your perceptions and other people's perceptions and views. We are spreading positivity instead of negative and unkind judgements. In this way, we continue the energy of other people's positive attributes to others. We are spreading kind thoughts, feelings, and actions.

♡ When you find yourself irritated, annoyed, uneasy about someone and want to say something negative about them to someone else, try to resist the urge to speak, be mindful and watch your thoughts, gently guide your thoughts to something positive about them, change your frame of mind and send them good wishes or say something nice about them. Everyone has qualities that we can learn from and that we can admire and use in our own lives. Concentrate on these qualities and spread the energy of these qualities to others.

♡ If you find yourself in the company of others who are talking negatively about someone else, just listen to them and then again gently guide your thoughts to a point where you can say something positive about them. Change the negative conversation into a more positive one. It does take a great deal of mindfulness and awareness to do this, especially when someone or a group of people's energy of negative judgements are strong; just listen first without reacting. Choose a day where you will listen and watch out for these sorts of conversations and practice for the whole day. You may not succeed straight away, but even if you remember yourself involved in a negative conversation about someone later on, you are on the right track to be able to transform it into something positive next time.

♈ If you find yourself thinking negative thoughts about someone else, check to see if you have ever done this kind of behaviour yourself, if so, rather than judge someone else, think of how you can change this behaviour in yourself.

It may take a great deal of practice and mindfulness to change our judgemental habits, but if we can concentrate on the positive we will feel the benefits. We can turn the conversation around, changing the perspective of the conversation into a positive one and passing on someone's good qualities to others which in turn will continue to be passed and spread onto many others, helping to change the negative perception of someone into gratitude and sending a positive wave of energy towards others.

Are you being Served?

"The best way to find yourself is to lose yourself in the service of others."
Mahatma Gandhi

Every day there are people in the background of our lives who provide a service of some kind; they make our life easier. They have taken the time to be trained in serving people and society. People such as grocers, restaurant workers, cleaners, people who work in the shops and supermarkets, medical staff, post people, dustbin workers, police officers, hairdressers, therapists, plumbers, gardeners, taxi drivers, the list goes on. All of whom put the time and effort into serving others and help make the world around us run more smoothly. What would we do without them, what would our life be without their service? Even though many of the people may be paid for their service in some way or another, we should still acknowledge how they help us and feel or express our appreciation and gratitude to them.

♡ Show gratitude for the human beings who make your life run smoothly. Start paying attention to the services we receive every day. Stop, notice and acknowledge the person who is doing it and take the time and opportunity to say thank you.

♡ If possible speak to the manager of the person or people who provide the service or write a note to them saying how grateful you are for the service a particular employee or employees gave you. Be specific about how they helped.

♡ Give someone or a group of people who provided a service a small gift. It could be handmade, fruit, flowers, food, chocolates or a cake, as a gesture of your gratitude for their service.

✎ Cards or notes are always a great way to show our appreciation. Write a little note of thanks or a "Thank you" card and give it to someone who you feel deserves appreciation for the service they provided. If could be a note from yourself or a group "Thank you" card, perhaps with a few words written in it of how grateful you are for their kind service. A grateful email or text message is also very thoughtful. They will not expect such a lovely gesture and it will surely make them feel very special and appreciated.

⚜ We can extend our gratitude to the objects and tools that people use to provide us with a service and which make our life easier. The shopping till machines, the plumbing tools, the medical equipment, the dustbin removal vans, the cleaning equipment, the kitchen tools, the gardening tools. If you look deeply you will start to notice the countless tools that are used every day when servicing; the people and their tools become one whole unit. Becoming aware of the tools that are used to help enhance our feelings of gratitude, we start to realise more and more that we are part of a community which supports each other, sharing the world, each playing our part to make it an easier, more comfortable and a safer place to live.

⚜ Look at the skills you have to provide a service that you are offering. Feel grateful for the skills needed to offer a service to others. Acknowledge its great worth and how you are very much part of a community that makes the world run more smoothly and harmoniously.

♡ Find ways in which you can be of more service or improve the service that you already offer. Be grateful for ideas from people on how you can improve your services, and what additional services that they would like to see.

♡ Start a group to offer a service where needed.

♡ Volunteer – offer your services to those in need. Look at the skills you already have to help others and those skills you'd like to learn and cultivate them to help serve others.

♡ Notice all the ways you are serving those you love every day. Notice how the people you love serve you every day. Feel grateful for these daily expressions of kindness and love.

☺ Thank your body for the many ways it serves you.

Watering the Flowers

"All the flowers of the tomorrows are in the seeds of today."
Indian Proverb

We all carry within us positive and beautiful qualities. These beautiful qualities are like seeds. Our mind and body are like a garden, and seeds within this garden when watered emerge and grow slowly into beautiful plants and flowers. It takes care, love, nurturing attention and gentle watering to help them grow.

The practice of watering the flowers is to recognise the beautiful qualities in someone and to express through words how you admire and appreciate these qualities. You could appreciate someone for a thoughtful act, a kind word, how they inspire you, their kindness, their understanding, how they were able to forgive, how they come through a difficult time in their life, how they have helped you through a difficult time in your life, how positive they are, how they see the good in others, how they helped someone or a group of people, how you admire their openness, how they make you laugh, their courage, their perseverance, their determination or simply their smile. There are many ways of seeing the good and positive qualities in a person.

Brighten someone's day. Acknowledge someone and water their positive seeds. In this way they will feel good about themselves, they will feel appreciated and valued for who they are. Watering their good seeds helps encourage other positive seeds within them to grow into even more beautiful flowers. Just as a lovely flower gives us joy, we also receive joy back from the flowers we've helped. The energy of gratitude we have projected out continues to touch the hearts of many others. Our expression of gratitude towards another person has a ripple effect.

♡ Choose someone in your life who you know well; a partner, parent, child, friend, work colleague, teacher. Whenever you feel the moment is right, water their good seeds. Make a conscious effort to see or look for something special about them or a quality you admire in them.

Oftentimes we keep what we feel inside us and are too shy to say anything. By making a conscious effort to practice watering the flowers, we can be more open with others. Saying something kind and positive to someone else will also make you feel better, the positivity and kindness that is projected flow in both directions. You could say something special spontaneously or you could arrange a time with a person you know well to water each other's good seeds. It's a wonderful way to give and receive positivity and keep your relationships blossoming beautifully.

♡ In our day-to-day lives we come across many people, those we've just met; strangers or acquaintances. If you get a sense of something positive about them that you'd like to say, don't keep it inside, water their flowers. Actively notice the goodness in others. Make a conscious effort to look for and see the positive in people, acknowledge it and say something. You will be sending out a wave of positive and grateful energy vibrations that lift the spirits of many.

♡ You possess many beautiful seeds. By watering your own seeds you learn to appreciate and love yourself. Don't wait or expect someone else to water your seeds, you can show yourself gratitude and appreciation at any time. Choose something now that you admire and respect about yourself; a quality you possess, or something you have done or said that you can be proud of. Water your flower; say it to yourself in your mind, out loud or write it down.

♡ For all of the practices above set a challenge to water someone's flowers every day. The watering the flowers practice can be done through spoken words or written down in a note, letter, card, email or text. When delivering your watering try and be as authentic as you can be; speak or write from your heart.

♡ This practice is done is a group where everyone in the group knows each other fairly well. Each person has a piece of paper on which they write their name at the top. The papers get passed from one person to the next, each person writing something special on it about the person, watering their flowers. At the end, each person has a list of lovely words written about them from everyone in the group.

Remember the Good

"Gratitude bestows reverence, allowing us to encounter everyday epiphanies, those transcendent moments of awe that change forever how we experience life and the world." John Milton

We all have had close relationships in our lives that are mixed with happy memories and not so happy memories. Whether our relationship is with our family, parents, siblings, children, friends or co-workers, the closer we are to people the more attached we become. We become attached for many reasons; we enjoy each other's company and enjoy doing different activities together, we share similar interests, we are there for each other, we share our thoughts and feelings with each other, we help and care about each other. Many close relationships last a lifetime, some we lose through a passing on, some break-up due to various reasons and some fade away due to changing circumstances. The important part of all close relationships is the sharing of a part of our lives with the other person, the sharing of our spirit. Many people with whom we have had a close relationship has altered and enhanced our lives in some way. We have taught each other, have been a guide for each other and have helped each other in some way.

When we are more attached to someone we can get upset with them for many different reasons. We may feel hurt and disappointed with each other's words or actions and then we show our unhappiness by getting angry or not speaking to them at all or holding onto the anger and resentment internally. Many of us hold onto hurts inside ourselves and carry them around, they come up now and then, are triggered by something or someone and we re-live the hurt over and over again. Sometimes we are able to speak to the other person about what the issue may be but many times we cannot speak to them at all and the differences are too great to resolve to mend the relationship. Someone close may have passed away or moved away and you may have been unable to resolve the hurt feelings you had towards them. Departing from any close relationship can be very painful for many reasons.

♡ If you have had a relationship which ended, try and remember all the good in that relationship. If the relationship didn't end well, don't dwell on the reasons why it ended, remember all the ways the relationship brought you happiness and joy. Nothing good is ever lost and we can transform any unpleasant experiences into something beautiful. If we look deeply we can see all the ways in which the relationship helped us. They may have taught us patience, compassion, forgiveness, understanding. There is always good to be found in any relationship. With all the difficulties which you may have encountered in the relationship, you learn something about yourself and them; you have grown in some way and benefited from each other's spirit.

♡ Look through a new perspective. See the person who you had a relationship with as someone who came into your life for a reason. They were sent to teach you, to bring out your greater qualities. Feel grateful for their part in your life and be grateful for your part in their life. During your relationship with someone, how did you help them?

👁 Think of someone now that you had a relationship with, someone who is no longer in your life. Close your eyes. Bring this person up in your mind's eye. Remember a happy moment with them. Visualise the scene and generate the feeling of happiness in the moment again within your heart. How do you feel remembering this moment or experience? What wonderful qualities are flowing from them? How do these qualities make you feel? Right within this memory; tell them how grateful you are to them for their presence, for knowing them, for being part of your life. Now wish them well wherever they may be in this moment, whether they are still alive or have passed away, or perhaps you don't know. Thank them and wish them peace and love.

✎ Write a peace note to someone or perhaps a group of people or an organisation you've been involved with which you have had issues with. Within your heart you've had trouble reconciling your differences and the hurt you've experienced during the relationship. To finally help set you free from the internal anger and resentment, send them your note of deep understanding, being honest with how you feel, helping them to understand you better and being grateful for how they've helped you.

The Wisdom of Our Teachers

"Better than a thousand days of diligent study is one day with a great teacher." Japanese Proverb

Teachers come in many different forms. Our teachers have been within us well before we were even born. Our genes are made up of generations of ancestors; we are born with inherited knowledge. All of our ancestors, their lives, culture, and experiences are within us and we carry their wisdom and direction throughout our lives.

Our parents or guardians are our teachers while we are growing up, guiding us along the way through life. Throughout our school life, we have many teachers; all have helped us to learn and understand the world around us. We learn so much from books; their authors are our teachers. Endless amounts of information can be found on the internet, instant learning at our fingertips. Friends can be great teachers. When we interact with many different people in our lives, we can learn from their experiences and the knowledge that they share with us. All our teachers help to broaden our minds and help us to understand and look deeply at the world and all that is within it and outside it. A great teacher can light a spark of passion within us to learn, a passion that will continue to grow inside us and open our minds and touch our hearts. We too can then pass on the knowledge we have learned onto others. Just as a pebble that drops in still water produces many ripples, knowledge continues endlessly from person to person.

The wisdom of great spiritual teachers has been passed down through generations to reach us; their wisdom shows us that our spirit is one with everything. We teach ourselves and others through our own innate wisdom and intuition. Nature and all that is within it is a beautiful teacher. We can learn from the many creatures, the trees, the rivers, the clouds and even a blade of grass. If you look carefully you will see that practically everything and everyone are our teachers, from a flower to the creatures on our Planet, to the stars and galaxies above us, we learn something from everyone and everything.

We go in search of teachers, some we energetically attract. We learn simply by observing others, most of the time people are completely unaware that we learning from them.

♡ Express thanks to your parents, grandparents or siblings for something special that they have taught you, directly or indirectly through their way of being.

♡ Think of a teacher from school, college or university who inspired you, who sparked a passion within you to learn. What warmed you to them – perhaps a special quality? What did you learn from them that has helped you in your life?

♡ Choose a favourite spiritual teacher or someone who you greatly admire from history. Choose one aspect of something that they have taught which you've put into practice in your life. How has their life story and wisdom helped you? What character trait that they have would you most like to instil in yourself?

♡ Think of a friend who has shared their knowledge or experience of something that has helped you in your life.

♡ Think of a book you loved reading. What was it that you loved about it and how has it helped you? Is there a particular character in a book that you can relate to and has taught you something?

�֎ What aspect of nature do you love? How can you become more aligned to the quality you admire?

🐾 Think of a creature that you feel drawn to. Why do you feel so close to it and is there something about its nature and life that you can learn from and gradually introduce into your own life?

🧘 What experiences from your past have been your greatest teachers?

🦋 Become more mindful and start to notice all the teachers in your life. Create your own special unique way of expressing your gratitude to them.

Stress or Heal

The nervous system is split into two parts. One activates the stress response and the other activates the healing response. Only one can be switched on at any one time as they need to perform their specific functions when activated.

The stress response also known as the fight-or-flight response is a physiological response to a perceived harmful event, attack or threat to survival. Most animal species on Earth have this instinct. It originates in the primeval part of the brain and is wired to be triggered quickly, without needing to be processed by thinking. The stress response triggers a cascade of stress hormones such as cortisol and adrenaline that produce well-orchestrated physiological changes; a rapid event on multiple bodily systems. The heart rate, respiratory rate, blood pressure, muscle tension, perspiration, narrow focus of attention and food-seeking attention (for energy) are all increased. Some things are decreased such as digestion and immune function; blood and energy are moved away from parts of the body needing repair and maintenance.

The stress response is an important protective mechanism but in today's modern life we are activating it for far longer periods than is necessary placing a serious toll on the body. A short burst of adrenaline gives us motivation and energy for the challenges in life, but a steady stream of it leads to chronic stress which plays a major role in many health challenges.

The healing response is the part of the nervous system that is responsible for cell repair, maintenance, proper digestive function, enhanced immune response, learning, and memory. It is the healing response that helps us maintain good health and wellness and it is this part of our nervous system that we should predominately live by. Making gratitude part of our way of being ensures that our body's healing response is steadily working to support us so we can live our lives fully with joy and happiness. All the practices in this book switch on the healing response, helping to boost the body ability to heal itself.

The body functions the same as it did 200,000 years ago but the world we live in today has changed considerably. The stress response will get triggered when the root emotion is fear. Some of the areas in which we experience fear are: work stressors such as being unhappy in our job, having a heavy workload or too much responsibility, working long hours, challenging work colleagues, loss of a job. Relationships stressors such as the death of a loved one, bereavement, unhealthy relationships, divorce, getting married, taking care of an elderly or sick family member, unable to communicate with family members, an expectation of ourselves and others. Financial worries such as an increase in financial obligations and debt. Health worries such as injury, illness or pain, negative beliefs about our health, worrying about the health of someone else. Life changes such as leaving home, moving to a new area or home, traumatic event, starting a family, new job. Social fears such as loneliness & social Isolation, competition. Other areas which we feel fear are unfulfilled dreams, pretending to be something that we're not, feeling out of touch with our life's purpose and feeling disconnected with our true spirit. All of these and much more can trigger the stress response in the mind and body suppressing many of the functions that our mind and body need to function well leading to some kind of imbalance and in most cases an illness of some sort.

☺ From the triggers above make a note of the ones that you are experiencing in your life. For each what one thing can you do to help yourself? Make a real effort to do it.

☺ Stress is in the mind's eye of the beholder. The impact of a stressful situation depends to a very large degree on your individual perception of the situation (how bad it is, how much control you have, whether you are expecting it, how optimistic you are about things getting better etc). A perception of gratitude can alter the way we interpret every situation in life helping to reduce the stress response considerably.

☺ Ask yourself when feeling stressed or anxious, what am I fearing? Why am I so fearful? You may find some of the roots of why you are feeling this way. In some situations where you are feeling nervous try and replace the emotion of fear with an emotion of excitement.

The Chemistry of Wellbeing

We know that stress and negative thought patterns can create a negative impact on our health and wellbeing. The opposite is also true, positive grateful uplifting thoughts have a healing effect on our health and wellbeing. The body has a natural healing mechanism. It can release a series of healthy, happy, healing chemicals when we increase our positivity, gratitude and engage in certain uplifting activities. Here are some of the chemicals that have a healing effect in our mind and body, and are responsible for making us feel good.

☺ Dopamine controls the brain's reward and pleasure centres. It is connected to learning and motivation and is released when we achieve a goal, giving us a surge of pleasure. Breaking down large goals into smaller ones helps to release dopamine more frequently. Challenging yourself with new goals, engaging in a new and creative hobby, appreciating and rewarding yourself, all release dopamine. When it comes to gratitude practices, keep it new and creative each time. Setting fresh goals for yourself will help release dopamine, appreciating and rewarding yourself in the process.

☺ Oxytocin is known as the love hormone, the cuddle chemical. It helps to strengthen relationships and promotes nurturing and relaxing sensations. Oxytocin is connected to feelings of love, trust, bonding, affection, attachment, and intimacy. It helps to boost the immune system and increases the health of the heart. Hugging, social activities, friendships, loving relationships, self-love, soothing music, listening and caring, receiving and expressing kindness, laughing, giving and receiving gifts, all increase the release of oxytocin into the body producing incredible healing effects. Bringing the feelings of gratitude into life in relation to all of these factors greatly enhances the release of oxytocin.

☺ GABA is a chemical that has a calming, relaxing effect on the mind and body helping to relieve stress and anxiety. Mindfulness, breathing exercises, positive thoughts, and gratitude practices help to naturally increase GABA in the body.

☺ DHEA is a chemical known as the *"fountain of youth"* as it's important in keeping our bodies healthy and strong. It helps us feel focused, energetic, dynamic, full of life and joy. Stress can deplete DHEA quite dramatically, as it does for all the other healthy, feel-good chemicals, so increasing our positivity, mindfulness and gratitude help keep DHEA in good balance.

☺ Serotonin is a natural mood stabiliser. It helps regulate anxiety and mood, sleep and appetite, memory and learning. Getting involved in a hobby you enjoy helps release serotonin into the body. Feeling significant and important, having a deep sense of meaning in your life and recalling happy moments and achievements also help release serotonin. Mindful gratitude practices help you achieve all of these.

☺ Nitric oxide is a very important chemical for the heart. It expands blood vessels, increasing blood flow, increasing oxygen and decreasing plaque growth and clotting. It has been shown that practising loving-kindness increases nitric oxide in the body. Being grateful certainly helps increase both love and kindness in our life.

☺ Endorphin is a natural painkiller which increases our sense of wellbeing and feelings of pleasure. Laughter, crying, listening to music, exercise, healthy foods and ultraviolet light can increase the release of endorphins into the body. An appreciation of all of these will help increase endorphins even further.

☺ Vasopressin is a chemical that is related to behaviour that enhances long-term relationships. The more grateful we are in our relationships the longer they will last as we are more content and happier.

☺ Gratitude is a practice that can dramatically enhance our health and wellbeing. Healthy foods, exercise, meditation, mindfulness, breathing exercises, ultraviolet light (being outside in the natural daylight for at least 20 minutes a day) all help to increase the healthy, healing chemicals released into the body, boosting our chemistry of wellbeing. A healthy balanced mix of these feel-good chemicals is essential to good health and wellbeing and generating the feelings of gratitude will ensure that they continue helping you.

The Two Minds

The best way to illustrate the concept of the two minds is by imagining an iceberg where only a small fraction about 5% is visible above the water represents the conscious mind and the larger proportion about 95% which is submerged represents the subconscious (or unconscious) mind.

A great analogy to help us understand the workings of the two minds' is to liken the subconscious mind to a computer hard drive where all the programs which allow the computer to function are stored. The conscious mind is the person who types on the keyboard to write the programs.

A human brain can process 400 billion bits of information per second; however, we are only conscious of 2,000 of those 400 billion bits. The subconscious mind can process 500,000 times more than what the conscious mind can. Most of the information of reality is processed by our subconscious mind.

The subconscious mind is the autopilot behind the conscious mind. It is where the mind stores away memories, experiences, beliefs and perceptions. From here come the thoughts, feelings, and emotions that shape our attitude, behaviour and mindset.

The subconscious mind is always communicating with the conscious mind and is what provides us with the meaning to all our interactions with the world, as filtered through our beliefs and habits. It communicates through feelings, imagination, sensations, and dreams.

As you can see the subconscious is a very powerful part of the mind, responsible for most of the things we are able to do in order to survive. However, the conscious mind can tap into the subconscious mind's power through mindful awareness.

🧘 Ask yourself - who is listening to the thoughts that are running through my mind? Those thoughts that are running in the background are coming from your subconscious mind. It is the conscious mind that's listening to it. Listen to your subconscious mind and to what it is trying to tell you. Liken your subconscious mind to a garden, and the conscious mind the gardener. The gardener can plant seeds of positive grateful thoughts into the garden. Mindfully be in the garden observing the life within it or pick the flowers and fruits of insights and intuition from the garden. The gardener can pull out the weeds (unhelpful patterns of thinking), and can clear the soil for planting new seeds (positive grateful patterns of thinking). What seeds do you want to plant and nurture and see grow and thrive in your garden?

Here is a list of the workings of the two minds and their main functions.

Conscious Mind	Subconscious Mind
Short-term Memory	Long-term Memory - Talking, eating, walking, driving
Makes Decisions	Monitors Body Functions -
Logic	Heart rate, digestion, breathing, healing
Intellectual	Records experiences through the five senses
Reasons	Records thoughts, emotions, beliefs and feelings
Rationalises	Emotional centre - Patterns & Feelings
Critical Thinking	Emotional reactions
Willpower	Conditional Responses
Analyses	Routine thoughts and feelings
Evaluates	Attitude, Beliefs, Perceptions & Values
Sets Goals	Prefers the Familiar
Judgement	Associative Memories
Speculates Possibilities	Protective Reactions
Creative Centre	Habitual / Hardwired Behaviours
New Ideas	Addictions
Learns from Mistakes	Skills
Intention	Runs on Autopilot
Attention	Home to our Intuition and Imagination
Focus & Concentration	Responds well to Visualisations
Regulates Behaviours & Reactions	Seat of Identity
Director	Resists Change
	Accepts information given to it

🧘 Become mindful and aware of the subconscious patterns that have helped you or are helping you and aware of those which are not helping you. Use and exercise as much of the conscious mind's function as possible to program habits, beliefs, patterns, attitudes, and perceptions that will help in you the in long-term. Make gratitude your second nature. If you practice it enough it will naturally flow from within your subconscious mind and help you throughout your life.

Neurons that Fire together Wire together

There are 100 billion neurons in the brain with 100 trillion neural connections. Neurons job is to transmit electrical and chemical signals. In 1949, Donald Hebb coined the phrase *"Neurons that fire together wire together"*. If we continually have thought patterns or do something, time after time, the neurons (cells) in our brain tend to strengthen that learning, becoming what we know as a "habit". The more we actually do of whatever we do, the more "habitual" that learning will become. Messages that travel the same pathway in the brain over and over again begin to transmit faster and faster. With enough repetition, they become automatic. That's why if we practice anything enough times, we can go on what they call "automatic pilot"; it becomes a subconscious action.

In order to positively increase the way our brain is circuited or wired up, we need to increase neural networks by forming habits for the things that we do want in life, rather than those that we don't; concentrate on the positives, rather than the negatives, in this way we become what we think. To become a more efficient learner, we have to discover how we learn best. By having a mixture of stimuli, appealing to our sensory receptors; our sight, sounds, tastes, smell, touch; we are far more likely to be able to learn more quickly, more efficiently and with the maximum recall.

Using creative methods of practising gratitude will help us learn better and generate positive habits, new patterns of thinking, feeling and behaving. Our brain cells will learn how to fire grateful thoughts and we will eventually with daily practice become naturally grateful. Thoughts and feelings of gratitude will automatically arise from our mind. Our perceptions that may not have been serving us in the past can be changed into a more positive attitude with enough practice.

This book is full of creative ideas for practising gratitude and tools for changing our habitual views and perceptions of the world into something positive and uplifting. Practising daily will help those neurons to wire together more efficiently. Repetitively keeping your practice creative and varied will motivate you to continue on the path.

Affirmations make you conscious of your thoughts. To affirm means to think or say something positive. It means to declare firmly and assert something to be true. When you say them or think them or even hear them, they become the thoughts that create your reality. Affirmations are proven methods of self-improvement because of their ability to rewire our brains. They raise the level of feel-good hormones and push our brains to form new clusters of "positive thought" neurons.

Every thought you think and every word you speak is an affirmation. All of our self-talk, our internal dialogue, is a stream of affirmations. You're using affirmations every moment whether you know it or not. You're affirming and creating your life experiences with every word and thought.

✎ If there is a habit that you wish to change or create, write down a description of the positive habit on pieces of paper and place them or stick them in various places where you will see them. If possible when you see the words read them out loud. Try and generate the feelings associated with what you have written, say and feel it with conviction.

♫ Choose a song that expresses words and emotions of a sentiment that you'd like to integrate into your life. Listen to it while having a shower, cooking, working, driving, meditating, sing along to it. Make it your affirmation. Absorb the meaning of the song into your mind, heart and body.

👁 Positive visualisations and creating mental images are a great way to retrain your brain. If you want to change a habit or manifest something in your life then visualise this happening together with the emotional energy of gratitude. Visualise that you already have a new positive habit, visualise your body being healthier, visualise the things you want to happen in your life. Generate the feelings of gratitude for them as if it has already happened. You are rewiring your brain cells which send signals to the rest of the cells in your body. Start to look for small pieces of evidence throughout your day that your affirmations, visualisations, and elevated emotions are manifesting. Through your thoughts, you are changing the vibration of the energy inside and around you to a positive one, which ultimately changes your reality.

Placebo or Nocebo Effect

"The ancestor of every action is a thought." Ralph Waldo Emerson

The placebo effect is the positive effect on a person's health and wellbeing, experienced after taking a placebo (a treatment or procedure). It is a mind-body phenomenon triggered by a person's belief in the benefit of a treatment working and their expectation of feeling better. A person's positive attitude, and faith play a huge role in the improvement of their health and wellbeing.

One of the most important factors that trigger expectations, belief and faith is verbal suggestion, trusting in the therapeutic practitioner. It is also intimately related to the ritual of the therapeutic act. Your own thoughts and feelings based on your innate beliefs are part of your own therapeutic ritual every single day of your life.

Extensive scientific investigation has been done on the placebo effect. It is now understood that small molecules called neurotransmitters and neuropeptides influence the activity of the brain and the body in specific ways. Neurotransmitters and neuropeptides are produced by our thoughts, feelings, and emotions which then act like keys turning the locks on different parts of the body switching on a particular function. If our thoughts, feelings, and emotions are positive it will considerably aid health recovery and maintenance. They perform an array of functions in the body such as repair, maintenance, production, balance, regeneration and boosting the immune function. Working in both directions, these molecules also influence our emotions positively, helping to increase feelings of wellbeing, creating cycles of positive mind-body, body-mind effects.

The opposite effect takes place when there is a negative expectation called the nocebo effect. A negative health effect is brought about by the negative expectation or belief, fuelling our thoughts, feelings, and emotions, triggering a flow of damaging messages from the brain to different parts of the body suppressing their functions creating health imbalances.

So, it is vitally important to use the power of our mind to help us with health challenges or prevent them. The human body is designed to heal, but it can only do so if we give it the right messages and maintain these messages by looking deeply at what we choose to believe.

Negative beliefs patterns create negative thought patterns; beating yourself up, feeling guilty, low self-value and confidence can send a series of negative messages into your cells. Your cells are listening to every thought you think. Eventually, cells start to deteriorate and the immune system can start attacking good cells as they are seeing them as a threat which eventually can cause inflammation in the body. Remember that it's your thoughts and beliefs that are important in any healing journey. We can choose whether to believe in a positive or negative statement. We create our own placebo and nocebo thought patterns all the time. Which one is going to benefit you? Many of the exercises in this book are sending a cascade of little molecular keys flowing into every part of your body, turned the locks of cells which then produce and perform amazing health-boosting functions. So practice as many as you can to keep those cells happy.

◉ You can liken a thought to a seed. You are the gardener who plants these seeds which contain the essence of your thoughts into the cells of your body. The cells then produce the flowers of the seeds you have planted. Close your eyes and focus on a particular area of your body that needs help. Use the power of your imagination and visualisation to create and generate powerful positive thoughts and feelings to this part of your body or the whole of your body. Make up a story, use images you love and send them to your body. Try and hold your concentration and focus for a few minutes. Do the same meditation or vary them every day maintaining the vibration of healing and love. There are now countless true stories of healing from this powerful mind-body connection.

☺ Watch out for the negative beliefs of other people and your own thoughts and words. We tend to see things as we are not things as they are. Knowing that every cell in your body is hearing what is thought and said, have more respect for them, change the limiting belief that fuels those thoughts, words, and actions. Your body will be grateful.

The Grateful Gene

"A man is but the product of his thoughts. What he thinks, he becomes."
Mahatma Gandhi

There are 50 trillion cells in the human body. Every cell in the body contains a nucleus, each nucleus houses the genes, and these genes contain the instructions, the blueprint, and the recipe for making proteins. Proteins are the building blocks of the body; they are responsible for the structure and function of the body. Proteins make up cells, which make up molecules, which make up tissues, which make up organs, which make up a human body. Proteins make up the immune system, hormones, and enzymes, they are needed to produce energy, carry oxygen and do countless other functions that are needed for a healthy body. Most genes are the same in all people, but a small number of genes (less than 1 percent of the total) are slightly different between people. These small differences contribute to each person's unique physical features.

Epigenetics is the study of how the expression of genes can be changed. The genes themselves cannot change, but how the gene is read by the cell to make different proteins are influenced by environmental factors such as diet, lifestyle choices, behaviours, and stress. Much scientific research has shown that our perception of the environment influences gene expression. How we perceive our surroundings whether it be harmonious or a threat can change the way our genes express themselves and what kind of proteins are made. Negative perceptions of the world around us can lead to the genetic expression of illness and positive perceptions of the world around us can lead to the expression of genes that promote healing, good health and wellness. Our perceptions influence our stress levels, diet, lifestyle choices, and behaviours. Therefore it is important to look deeply at the way we interpret our surroundings and experiences and how we choose to live our life.

The positive practices of gratitude change our whole perception or interpretation of the world, turning even very difficult life challenges and experiences into something we can learn and grow from.

Gratitude dramatically changes the lens through which we see ourselves and the world around us. Our internal world knows only how to express itself according to the messages that it receives from our perceptions of the outside world. These messages or signals flow directly to our genes which then express themselves according to the signals that were sent to them. It is therefore very important that we send messages of gratitude to our genes so that they express themselves in a way to promote our health and wellbeing. Studies have shown how the antibody IgA, which fights bacteria and viruses, boosts the immune system functions considerably better when gratitude is regularly practiced. Many more studies have been done to show how highly positive expressions of emotion such as gratitude, love, compassion, inspiration, and kindness enhance our health and wellbeing and promote healthy gene expression, increasing the health and function of our cells to protect us against disease. Studies have shown that after 90 days of practices such as gratitude, meditation, positive thinking, lifestyle changes, mindfulness, mind-body-spirit practices, 500 genes for health were switched on and expressed.

👁 In meditation think of something you are grateful for, feel it fully in your mind and heart. Holding this feeling of what you are grateful for, visualise sending this message into your body. You can visualise the message as coloured light, or liquid, or anything that conveys your gratitude in the most creative way possible. Start with choosing an organ; travel into the tissue that makes up the organ, travel even further into one of the millions of molecules that make the tissue, and then choose one of the cells that make up the molecule. Once you have reached the membrane (outer skin) of the cell send your message of gratitude through the outer layer into the nucleus at the centre of the cell, the home of the genetic material, see the genes light up, signalling that they received your wonderful message of gratitude. Now see all the cells in your body light up with your grateful message.

☺ Reprogram your genetic expression from negative to positive, from illness to wellness. Change the way you interpret things, people, experiences, and the environment around you. View things in a healthier light. Rebalance your perception and send your genes the instructions to express themselves positively.

The Mirror Effect

We are all intrinsically connected with one another. Thoughts, feelings, emotions and actions travel from one person to another, they are contagious. You may have noticed how someone's mood can affect you. In most cases, we are unaware of how the vibrations of someone or a group of people affect our own thoughts, feelings, emotions, and behaviour.

Positive expressions such as kindness, love, courage, joy, happiness, gratitude, co-operation, inspiration flow from person to person. Just one positive word, smile, action can have a ripple effect on thousands of people. This effect is due to mirror neurons in the brain which cause us to subtly copy the expressions, actions and behaviours of those around us. Mirror neurons are essential for social interactions, empathy, imitation, and emulation; they are a fundamental tool in the learning process. We are social beings; our survival depends on our understanding of the actions, intentions, emotions, and feelings of others. Without attachment and protection, the human species wouldn't have survived.

Mirror neurons are activated in the brain when watching an action, allowing us to adopt another person's point of view and imitate and emulate other people's actions.

Empathy mirror neurons dissolve the barrier between you and others, which gives another example of how we are all connected with each other. Everyone's mirror neurons are constantly talking to each other.

Babies reproduce facial expressions, we cry while watching a sad movie, laughter, smiling, yawning is contagious; we feel someone else's emotional pain, when we see someone being touched, our own touch receptors are activated. From birth, we learn how to eat, speak and dress by copying the actions of other's. Throughout our whole lives, our mirror neurons help us learn, interact and empathise.

They enable us to reflect body language, facial expressions, and emotions. They are key to child development, as well as relationships and education. Humans are social beings programmed to learn from others. Watching someone gives us a tangible experience of learning.

Our emotional state of mind is expressed through our face which is copied by other's subtly affecting their mood; this mood then get passed onto other's and the stream of positivity continues on and on. This of course, works with negativity as well. A negative emotional state can spread just as fast through the web of consciousness.

We are all inextricably interconnected. We are all contributing to the web of life. It is our thoughts that create our words and our actions. Understanding that just one thought can have consequences on thousands of people and ultimately the world, it is so important to create positive thoughts which encourage positive words, actions, and expressions, helping to inspire and create a kind, loving and grateful world. We can create an endless ripple of gratitude.

🧘 We have seen through history how one person can affect thousands, even millions of people. Some created ripples of fear, some created ripples of love. Think of someone you admire that created ripples of love and gratitude. Learn more about them; their childhood, upbringing, what inspired them to create change, what did they do to create change in themselves, in others and the world.

♡ Think of someone is your own life that you admire that has produced a ripple of loving energy though just one word, action or behaviour.

♡ How have you created ripples of change? Think of an act of kindness, a grateful word that has spread amongst a large group of people.

♡ Every time you practice, through thought, feeling, word or action know within your heart that you are not only experiencing it yourself but that hundreds, thousands even millions of people are affected by it. Imitate happy, positive and inspiring people. Become mindful of what you do, say and feel around others, knowing that people are picking up on everything do. When we experience another person's action as our own, it helps us understand them. We pick up and reflect other people's emotions. What emotions do you want to pick up and pass on?

The Fountain of Youth

"Let the beauty of what you love be what you do." Rumi

Built into every cell of our body is the "fountain of youth" called telomeres. Telomeres are parts of DNA, attached at the end of our chromosomes forming an extension of the DNA. Every time the DNA is copied, a process that is happening all the time due to cell division, repair and renewal, the telomeres are shortened. Eventually, the DNA is copied so many times, the telomeres run out and start cutting off pieces of the genes. This causes disease and the aging process as genetic information for healthy regeneration is now lost.

The good news is that an enzyme called telomerase adds extensions to the telomeres so that it gets longer to allow cellular division, repair and renewal to happen without DNA damage as it maintains the integrity of the genes to carry out their functions efficiently. Telomerase helps maintain good health and increases our longevity.

What activates telomerase and what inhibits telomerase? You know by now that the mind, lifestyle choices, nutrition, and exercises practices have a powerful effect on our health and wellbeing. Our life conditions and experiences have an enormous impact on how we perceive ourselves and the world, therefore impacting the messages that our cells receive. The "fountain of youth" enzyme responds favourably to having a meaningful purpose in life as it sends messages to the body that you love what you do, you love the environment you live in, your love the people around you, you are being of service, you love life, you are grateful and very importantly you value and appreciate yourself. This positive attitude activates telomerase helping to enhance your life and therefore increase your longevity.

What is your purpose? The first step to finding your purpose is to understand how you best impact others and then look for ways you can create opportunities to help increase the impact.

Your life purpose is not what you should, or should not do; it is not governed by the patterns you are used to, ones that have been programmed into you during your life. It's not about the expectations of others. Your purpose is what brings out the most of your potential in the world. It is a bridge between your unique gifts and what the world wants most from you. It's your own unique truth, expressing your essence that allows you to live creatively and find meaning in every moment. You'll find that your purpose is as much about the world, the people you love and the community you live in as it is about yourself. Our happiness is hugely dependent on how we connect with, and contribute, to others. Allow the narrative of your life to transform problems into opportunities unfolding more of your life purpose. Your life purpose can become a new story that opens up a world of possibility to you. Ask yourself these questions to discover your purpose.

- What keeps you going when life is hard?
- What was the most rewarding thing you have ever done for someone else and why was it so rewarding?
- How do others describe your impact on their life?
- If you had all the time in the world to volunteer, who would you volunteer for? What or who would you like to support? What do you care deeply about?
- When you look back on all these years, what do you want to remember? Imagine talking with your future self. 1, 5, 10 years from now, what will you want to look back on? What will you remember? How would you like to be remembered?
- What moments in your life have given you feelings of great love, deep satisfaction, or purpose?
- How have you contributed to the wellbeing of others?
- What are the greatest problems you have encountered in your life? In overcoming them, what talents, gifts, and ideas have you developed?
- What activities most inspire you?
- Thinking back to your early life, what did you love to do, what gave you the most joy and happiness?
- Taking money out of the picture, what would you do to feel most fulfilled and most alive? How would you use your insights, experiences, and gifts to bring more love into the world?

Postcards from the Subconscious

Our dreams while we are asleep send us messages from our subconscious. On waking sometimes we remember them vividly and sometimes we forget them. The dreams we remember seem so real as if we had actually experienced them. The body does not know the difference between an experience and a thought. So if the dream seems real, we have experienced it, which is why we feel the emotions that go along with the experience. We can clearly understand some of the dreams we've had as they are related to something that has been on our minds, but most times our dreams are a mystery, we cannot fathom their meaning. Our dreams have a purpose; they are trying to tell us something from our deep inner mind and heart.

🧘 Before you go to sleep, just before you are dropping off, say to yourself "I will remember my dreams". First thing on waking, ask yourself if there is any part of a dream that you can remember. If you do remember something, what was it? Remember as much detail as you can, what were your emotions during the dream? Some dreams can be pleasant and some unpleasant. Try and understand the message within the dream. What do you feel your deep subconscious is trying to tell you? Is there something within it that you can feel grateful for – an experience, a feeling, a lesson, an emotion, a message for you to steer your life in a certain direction? Before you drop off you can say to your subconscious "I wish to dream of something I am grateful for or something I need to be grateful for". Drop any message into your subconscious, like sending a postcard to it, and then allow your dreams to send back its own postcard with a message to help you onto a grateful path.

🧘 We can remember the essence of some of the dreams we've had in our past, some going back to childhood. Somehow we are still able to remember them. Remembering a pleasant dream, generate the feelings of gratitude for the sleep time experience. You may like to share your dream experience with someone, describing it to them in as much detail as you can remember.

Focus & Attract

The reticular activating system (RAS) is in the base of the brain. The RAS acts as a filter against all the data that is around us, such as sounds, images, tastes, colours, pictures. There can be up to 2,000,000 bits of data at any time. The brain can only process so much at a time. So, the RAS 'filter' only lets things through that it thinks is important. So how does it know what is important? By what you focus on most. It takes what you concentrate on and develops a filter to it. It sorts through the data and delivers only the parts that are essential to you.

The Reticular Activating System helps you see what you would like to see and in doing this, influences your actions. If you concentrate hard on your objectives, your RAS will uncover the individuals, data and opportunities that help you achieve them. If you love positivity, you will become more aware of and look for positivity. Have you noticed that when you make a carefully thought out decision to buy a specific brand and type of car you start seeing those automobiles everywhere you go? Focus on the negative things, and you will invite pessimism and problems into your life. Concentrate on the great, and they will come to you because your brain is seeking them out. It's not magic; it's your Reticular Activating System affecting the world you observe around you.

Depending on whether your self-talk is positive or negative, the RAS will start to show you things to prove that your new belief is true for you. The more proof you see, the stronger your belief that it is true. The stronger your belief is, the more you are likely to tell yourself it. Self-talk leads to proof which leads to a belief which then continues in a circle as your belief will help fuel your self-talk, which means we get what we expect.

☺ Choose to focus on the positive aspect of things and make positive statements about yourself. Your RAS will then know what it needs to focus on and you'll attract more of it into your life. We attract something because we choose to focus on it, both positive and negative. Notice how changing your focus changes what you attract. Experiment with it and see what unfolds.

Higher Vibrations

"Everything in life is vibration. Everything is energy and that is all there is to it. Match the frequency of the reality you want and you cannot help but get that reality. It can be no other way. This is not philosophy, this is physics." Albert Einstein

The human body is made up of organs, which are made from tissue, which are made of cells. There are an estimated 50 trillion cells in the human body. Each cell is made up of molecules and the molecules are made up of atoms. Within each cell, there are an estimated 100 trillion atoms. Atoms are made up of smaller subatomic particles, called electrons, protons and neutrons. The nucleus at the centre of the atom is around 100,000 times smaller than the atom that it's housed in. If the nucleus were the size of a peanut, the atom would be about the size of a football field. If we lost all the empty space inside our atoms, we would each be able to fit into a particle of dust, and the entire human species would fit into the volume of a sugar cube. 99.9999999999999 of every atom is known as empty space, but this empty space inside an atom is not really empty, it looks like a physical void. Atoms are mostly made out of invisible energy, not tangible matter. Atoms are like tiny bells that vibrate. Quantum physicists discovered that physical atoms are made up of vortices of energy that are constantly spinning and vibrating, each one radiating its own unique energy signature. Therefore we are really beings of energy and vibration, radiating our own unique energy signature. Since everything in the universe is made up of atoms, Einstein has rightly pointed out that everything in life is vibration, is energy. The solid world we see around us is a manifestation of how this energy field interacts.

It has been shown through countless scientific studies and research that different states of emotion, perception, and feelings result in different electromagnetic frequencies. Studies have shown that positive emotions and operating from a place of peace within oneself can lead to a very different experience for the person emitting those emotions and for those around them. When we enhance our internal state we impact the external world around us and influence how others feel as well.

Like attracts like. When we are mindful of each moment and exist in the harmonious state of gratitude, our blessings multiply. When we can acknowledge and feel the gratitude for whatever we have or experience we change our own vibrational frequency. Whatever vibrational energy we cultivate and give out is the same vibrational energy that we will attract more of into our lives. The energy we ripple out in our thoughts and actions attracts energy back of a similar frequency. Gratitude has its own vibrational frequency that draws more to you and so more to be grateful for comes into your life. When we live in gratitude, our giving becomes receiving. Gratitude has a vibration and it can change the vibration of everything that surrounds it. When we feel and express gratitude we not only elevate our own vibration but the vibration of what we are grateful for. This higher frequency also projects itself into the future, attracting more for us to be grateful for.

☺ There are several ways we can raise our vibrational energy -

- Count your blessings – cultivate a grateful heart
- Recognise and appreciate beauty wherever you go
- Practice kindness and give from your heart
- Spend time with loved ones
- Sing joyful uplifting songs
- Move your body – exercise, yoga, tai-chi, dance, play
- Listen to music that inspires and uplifts you
- Create something – art, cooking, dance, music, writing
- Breathe mindfully. Practice deep breathing
- Connect with nature. Spend quality time in the great outdoors
- Meditate – stilling your mind and body
- Practice present-moment mindful awareness
- Smile, Laugh, Hug, Love
- Practice self-love and appreciation
- Open your heart – send loving-kindness to others and yourself
- Contentment – you have everything you need
- Deep understanding – the interconnectedness of everything
- Share your time, energy and skills with others
- Speak well of others – use kind, wise and inspiring language
- Practice as many of the practices suggested in this book

Rewrite your History

"The secret of change is to focus all of your energy, not on fighting the old, but on building the new." Socrates

So-called bad memories can trouble people for years and can contribute to negative views of themselves in the present and to health challenges as mind and body are so inextricably linked. What if those negative memories of the past could somehow be revised in consciousness? You can't change the actual events themselves, but perhaps you can look at them differently and in a more adaptive manner for your feelings of wellbeing. We can have a desire to change the past for the sake of a better future. An effective way to do this by rescripting the image, edit negative memories via imagination which leads to a happier ending.

In imagery rescripting you edit negative memories via imagination, which leads to a "happy ending" as you send your adult self back to the time of the bad experience in an effort to "comfort or defend" yourself. You don't actually erase that memory, but you store it away in a revised fashion that competes with, and hence weakens, the power of the original memory. Through positive mental imagery, you can feel more in control, less helpless, and less despairing about yourself and your life.

Imagery's powerful ability to revise and thus negate bad memories stems in part from the fact that your memories are often perceptual. In other words, you don't just think about the bad event, you see it in your mind's eye. Those images serve to increase the impact of whatever words you attach to the memory.

The chosen memory each of us holds in our minds determines the story of our past. Unfortunately, they are seldom an accurate portrayal of what really happens at any given time. Instead, the majority of our memories are a process that we use to make meaning and sense of our experiences. But with most of that process unconscious, the quality of both our past and our future reflects the stories we habitually focus on and tell.

Our memories all begin with our sensory perception. We like to believe we know and observe everything going on around us all the time, but we actually only perceive a tiny percentage of the input happening at any given moment. Of course, consciously and unconsciously we pre-guide our minds to primarily pay attention to things we believe are important, unique, or threatening. The remaining thousands of bits of input are then lost in an instant.

Still, what we later recall isn't really the exact observation. Instead, what we store is the overall general idea of the memory, the "gist" of the story, based upon how we choose to interpret it. Even when we manage to hang on to a few of the more important details, what we really recollect is even well-intentioned people making a sincere effort to be accurate will inadvertently fill in the gaps by making things up. People will believe the memories they make up.

When we repeatedly tell our interpretation of the story and then recall it at a later date, there wasn't just memory loss; there were also memory additions. With time we tend to smooth out our memories and fit them into a comfortable narration that fits our prior knowledge of the world. It is very human to want to find meaning and make sense of the world and our experiences. So, when we remember, we rewrite our memories into a story to fits our prior knowledge and beliefs, and even our preformed tendencies and bias.

☺ Choose to remember, and then tell, a better story about your past. What we individually choose to focus on, highlight, and repeatedly tell others, and ourselves, can either lead to a happier life or reinforce the past negatively. When you find yourself sifting through your images of the events in your past that cause you to feel regret or sadness, encourage yourself to challenge not only your assumptions about yourself and your past but even the visual memories. Work to alter them in a proactive and positive way to rewrite your past and then create a better future. With practice and focus you can effectively train your brain and sensitise it toward the positive on a regular basis. With effort, it is possible to rewrite your experiences and memories in ways that bring you more peace, happiness, and meaning.

Serendipity & Synchronicity

"Live life as if everything is rigged in your favour." Rumi

Serendipity is usually defined as the gift of making fortunate discoveries by accident. These amazing opportunities are often referred to as meaningful coincidences or moments of pure luck. Serendipity can also be those events in life which initially seem unfavourable, though in hindsight we realise how fortunate we are to have experienced them.

Some people feel serendipity is a fated circumstance since it happens when you are striving for one thing only to gain something entirely different. When you experience a setback, trust that it is happening to guide you to something better. When facing something that appears to be less than perfect, know that it is happening for a reason and expect something greater will evolve from the situation.

Given that a serendipitous event is unplanned and unanticipated, the moment could potentially be missed or overlooked by one person, while the same event discovered and developed by another. According to research, lucky or serendipitous people generate their own good fortune by virtue of the way they view life. People with optimistic qualities are more likely to benefit from chance events and turn serendipity into opportunity.

Synchronicity has a close relationship to serendipity as the word itself means synchronised in time, a co-incidence; incidences happening together. Examples are thinking of someone and they call you, thinking of something or having an intention and somehow it manifests, a wish comes true, when improbabilities come together. Synchronicity is when several events conspire together seemingly unrelated and yet when they meet together they form a pattern or bring us the result or the solution that we were looking for. We've all had the occasion when a whole series of things seem to conspire together into a happy coincidence to bring us the goal, solution or the thing we were looking for.

Again we need to be aware of synchronicities to turn them into opportunities and allow more synchronous and serendipitous moments to occur. The more we experience them and appreciate them the more they will get repeated. We experience what we expect.

🧘 Become grateful for all the coincidences, synchronicities and serendipities; guided messages from the universe. Be open to this guidance; look for signs in your everyday life. You may want to set an intention and see what messages or experiences come from it. Smile at those moments when you thought of something, wished for something and it happened or maybe something entirely different happens that takes you by surprise but you see the messages and opportunities in them. You trust that you are being guided to a place of change, growth, and renewal. We must try and see everything that happens in life as an opportunity.

♡ Share with others your moments of serendipity and synchronicity so that they too can discover their own moments.

🧘 Notice the little serendipitous moments that permeate life. Green lights, something dropped but it didn't break, just catching the train.

🧘 Increase your chances of experiencing serendipitous and synchronous moments using these methods.

- Create and notice chance opportunities.
- Make lucky decisions by listening to your intuition.
- Create self-fulfilling prophecies via positive expectations.
- Adopt a resilient attitude that transforms bad luck into good.
- Do something out of the ordinary. Change your normal routine.
- Become passionate about your dreams, drawing to you opportunities to make them happen.
- Recognise the silver lining. Every moment is a learning opportunity; everything we experience contributes something to your understanding of the world and yourself.

Serendipity and synchronicity can change your life in ways you may never have dared to dream; it's just a matter of remembering to welcome these moments into your life and to make the most of them.

Reflections of Gratitude

"Give thanks for a little and you will find a lot." Nigerian Proverb

Here are some questions to help generate appreciation.

- ❖ Who is always there for you, and how do you feel about them?
- ❖ What made you laugh or smile today?
- ❖ What's the weather like today, and what's one good thing about that?
- ❖ What one kind or thoughtful thing did someone do for you recently?
- ❖ What something are you looking forward to in the future?
- ❖ What's the most beautiful thing you saw today?
- ❖ What simple pleasures did you enjoy, or can you enjoy today?
- ❖ How have you used your talents and abilities recently, and what have you enjoyed about doing that?
- ❖ Has anyone done anything recently that made your job easier?
- ❖ How has technology enhanced your life and your connections recently?
- ❖ What are three things your arms or legs allow you to do that you enjoy?
- ❖ What something have you witnessed recently that reminded you that people are good?
- ❖ What one thing have you experienced recently that made you feel a sense of wonder or awe?
- ❖ How many of your basic needs do you not need to worry about meeting today?
- ❖ What's something that inspired or touched you recently?
- ❖ Who have you enjoyed being around recently, and why?
- ❖ What have you seen in nature recently that made you feel happy, peaceful, or free?
- ❖ Have you had an opportunity to help someone recently, and how did you feel about that?
- ❖ What choices have you made in the last five years that you'd thank yourself for making?
- ❖ What's something you have easy access to that always improves your mood, and how has it improved your life?
- ❖ What something did you do well recently, and what qualities or skills enabled you to do this?
- ❖ Looking back at a past experience that was challenging, what resources do you have now that you did not have back then?

- ❖ What something have you witnessed recently that reminded you that life is good?
- ❖ What's improved about your life from this time last year?
- ❖ What modern conveniences (e.g. electronics and appliances) do you enjoy that make your life easier?
- ❖ How has modern medicine or alternative medicine improved your life, recently or overall?
- ❖ What movie, book, blog, or article affected your life for the better recently?
- ❖ What's the last thing you enjoyed with your senses?
- ❖ How do your friends and/or family members show they care about you?
- ❖ What's the last song you heard that you enjoyed? How did it make you feel, and why?
- ❖ What have you learned recently that will help you in the future?
- ❖ Can you think of any non-physical gifts you've received recently – someone's time, attention, understanding, or support?
- ❖ Think of someone who always really listens when you talk, and how does that affect you?
- ❖ What did not exist 10, 20, 50 years ago that is a regular part of your daily life now?
- ❖ Tap into your senses: What do you love to eat? What do you love to look at? What do you love to smell? What do you love to hear? What do you love to touch?
- ❖ What is comfortable about this moment?
- ❖ What did your mother, husband, brother, sister, child, … do today without you having to ask for it?
- ❖ What were you thanked for today?
- ❖ What did you learn today that has helped you or will help you and someone else?
- ❖ What is happening inside your body at this moment?
- ❖ What perception did you have today which you can see from a different angle?
- ❖ What can I change about myself to make the world a better place?
- ❖ What would be your greatest teaching?
- ❖ What qualities about another person do you admire the most and would like to emulate in your own life?
- ❖ Ask yourself "How are you feeling right now?".

Think up some more questions to ask yourself and others.

The Miracle of Life

"Each second of life is a miracle." Thich Nhat Hanh

🧘 What created life? What does it mean to be alive? What is it that's keeping us alive? If we can ponder over the answers to these questions, we will certainly be left with a feeling of complete and utter awe at the miracle of life within us and all around us. Everything that exists is alive. For anything to be in existence it required infinite conditions and factors to bring about its life. This includes ourselves, other species, nature all around us and every single object that we see and use around us. Inanimate objects seem to appear as if they have no life just because they do not move, but the very fact that they exist, means they are alive, they have a purpose. Look around you now and place your eyes on an object. Ask yourself – is there life in the object? Can I find something to be grateful for in this object?

🧘 What created life? Look at all the factors involved in creating the life within and all around you. How did it all begin? What was the spark that initiated it all? They say the Big Bang created life, but what came before the big bang? What was the force that created life? It must be some form of intelligence as it seems highly unlikely that everything in the universe was created by random chance. This force has been given many names – The Source, God, Higher Consciousness, Life Force, Quantum Field, and many other names. We can become connected to this energy that created life by becoming aware and grateful for it within ourselves and within everything around us. In this connection, we find what it is to be truly alive. Everything is an expression of life. We are intrinsically woven together. Look at all the factors within ourselves, our own body that is keeping us alive, giving us life. The heart beating, the breath, the digestive system, the immune system, the senses, the countless mechanisms in all of our systems made up by trillions of cells in the body working continuously inside us keeping us alive without any effort from ourselves. What is it that's doing all of this for us, giving us this beautiful life? The same applies to everything in nature and everything around us. Each second of life truly is a miracle when we connect to it and are grateful for it. Make the most of every precious moment.

I am grateful

I would love to hear about your gratitude practices. Let me know how you are getting on. Please share your insights and what you have learned and experienced from trying out some of the practices in this book.

Please share your experiences by email at -

gratefulwellbeing@gmail.com.

- ❖ Do you have a particular favourite gratitude practice?
- ❖ Have you noticed any changes in your own life after you've started practising gratitude?
- ❖ Which perceptions that you previously held have changed after a particular practice?
- ❖ How have you shared your practice with others?
- ❖ What/Who do you value much more now?
- ❖ How has your practice inspired others?
- ❖ What have you attracted into your life after starting to practice gratitude?
- ❖ What you are grateful for in the future?
- ❖ What challenging experience from the past or present are you viewing differently now because of your gratitude practice?
- ❖ Tell me about a gratitude ceremony or ritual that you've created.
- ❖ If you have created something out of your practice, I'd love to see a photo of it.
- ❖ Share with me any of your answers from the many questions asked in this book.
- ❖ Has any health issue improved from practising gratitude?
- ❖ How has practising gratitude enhanced your relationships with yourself, other people, and the world around you?
- ❖ Create your own gratitude practice. Something you have thought up yourself. I'd love to hear about it and your experiences practising it.

I look forward to hearing from you. Thank you for reading this book.
I wish you a very happy grateful journey through life.

Acknowledgments

♡ Thank you to my parents. I am deeply grateful for your love and support throughout my life. I love you both very dearly.

♡ Thank you to my dear husband Steve who is my loving friend and companion through life. I am so grateful for your warm and loving heart, and your wonderfully inspiring insights. Thank you for being so encouraging and for always supporting me. I love you.

♡ Thank you to the Sangha (a global mindful community which practice the teachings of Thich Nhat Hanh). Thank you everyone at Plum Village. I am truly grateful for all the beautiful practices that we share together.

♡ Thank you to the Bhrama Kumaris (World Spiritual University) and all my dear friends within our community. I am deeply grateful for your unlimited source of wisdom, love, and understanding.

♡ Thank you to all my dear friends and my lovely parents-in-law. You are my wonderful extended family. I am grateful and feel blessed to share the experience of life with you. I dearly love you all.

♡ Thank you to all the inspiring teachers around the world who help cultivate health and wellness. Thank you to all the people who spread the teachings of peace, love, understanding, and gratitude. I feel blessed to be part of a larger family, a growing community of people who are helping, educating, guiding and inspiring others to connect with their true selves.

♡ Thank you to nature and to this incredible gift of life, to the divine energy that gives life to all. I am truly grateful and feel deeply blessed.

♡ Thank you to Marie Birkinshaw for kindly editing this book. Your knowledge and experience as a book editor has helped tremendously. I am very grateful for all the time and energy you spent editing the book.

♡ Thank you to all the readers of this book. Happy grateful journey!

About the Author

Falguni Patel is a qualified yoga teacher, nutritional therapist, and a mindfulness and gratitude practitioner. She lives in Loughborough, UK, where she runs her own holistic health and wellness practice called Grateful Wellbeing.

Her fascination with holistic therapies started at a very young age. Over many years she used a natural and alternative approach to help her overcome various health and life challenges and is now passionate about sharing her knowledge and experience and educating others on ways to nurture body, mind, and spirit through nutrition, yoga, mindfulness and gratitude practices.

Born in India, raised in Kenya and the UK, Falguni has a great love for travel, photography, gardening, astronomy, cooking, arts, natural history, holistic therapies, wildlife, nature, walking and spending time with her family and friends.

For more information visit – www.gratefulwellbeing.com

Bibliography & Further Reading

- Thich Nhat Hanh, 'The Miracle of Mindfulness', Beacon Press, 1991
- Steindl-Rast, David, 'A Good Day: A Gift of Gratitude', Sterling Ethos, 2013
- Tolle, Eckhart, 'The Power of Now', New World Library, 1999
- Hay, Louise, 'You Can Heal Your Life', Hay House, 1984
- Dyer, Wayne, 'The Power of Intention', Hay House, 2005
- Dispenza, Joe, 'Breaking the Habit of Being Yourself', Hay House, 2013
- Lipton, Bruce, 'The Biology of Belief', Hay House, 2015
- Hamilton, David, 'It's the Thought that Counts', Hay House, 2009
- Winfrey, Oprah, 'The Wisdom of Sunday', Bluebird, 2017
- Shivani, Sister, 'Happiness Unlimited', Pentagon Press, 2015
- Rankin, Lissa, 'Mind over Medicine', Hay House, 2013
- Choquette, Sonia, 'Trust your Vibes', Hay House, 2005
- Turner, Kelly A, 'Radical Remission', Bravo Ltd, 2015
- George, Mike, 'Mindsets', Mike George, 2015
- Cousins, Norman, 'Anatomy of an Illness', W.W. Norton & Co, 1996
- Gandhi, Mahatma, 'Gandhi: An Autobiography', Beacon Press, 1993
- Mandela, Nelson, 'Long Walk to Freedom', Abacus, 2013
- Keller, Helen, 'The Story of My Life', Dover Publications, 2012

Recommended Websites

- www.plumvillage.org
- www.brahmakumaris.org
- www.drjoedispenza.com
- www.drwaynedyer.com
- www.louisehay.com
- www.gratefulness.org
- www.eckharttolle.com
- www.brucelipton.com
- www.drdavidhamilton.com
- www.greggbraden.com
- www.heartmath.com
- www.kriscarr.com
- www.relax7.com